Crossing the Bridge

CROSSING THE BRIDGE

The Missing Link in the Dialogue about Difference

Carrie Gibson

Tucson, Arizona

CROSSING THE BRIDGE: THE MISSING LINK IN THE
DIALOGUE ABOUT DIFFERENCE

Copyright © 2003 by Carrie Gibson. All rights reserved.
Printed in the United States of America.

Published by Fenestra Books
610 East Delano Street, Suite 104
Tucson, AZ 85705, USA

No part of this book may be used or reproduced in any manner whatsoever without written permission, except in the case of brief quotations in critical articles and reviews.

International Standard Book Number: 1-58736-214-7
Library of Congress Control Number: 2003106465

Cover design and art work by Michael Braden
Copyright © 2003

*To Michael, my partner, my editor in life, and my love;
to Elsa and Jamie, my inspirations to keep
growing, playing, and loving;
and to Edmonia, who told me to "get to work" on my passion.*

Contents

Acknowledgements ix
Preface—The Case for Diversity. xi

Chapter One—Where Did I Begin? Or, Why Me? 1
Chapter Two—Exercising the Imagination. 13
Chapter Three—Fast Forward to Who Am I Really,
 and the Tool 21
Chapter Four—No Problem Here 39
Chapter Five—Applying Imagination to the Big Picture. 47
Chapter Six—Connecting with Emily. 53
Chapter Seven—Hitting Too Close to Home 61
Chapter Eight—Our Attachment to Irritation 65
Chapter Nine—Bridging a Polarity 69
Chapter Ten—The "I Love My Opinions" Obstacle 75
Chapter Eleven—I'll Save You, Nell 81
Chapter Twelve—To Be PC or Not to Be PC 87
Chapter Thirteen—The "If Only" Moments. 93
Chapter Fourteen—It's the Little Things 97
Chapter Fifteen—To Do It or Not to Do It. 103
Chapter Sixteen—How to Practice the Tool of Imagining. 109
Chapter Seventeen—Will the Technique of Imagining
 Cure Me of My Prejudices?. 117
Chapter Eighteen—Whadaya Mean, No? 119
Chapter Nineteen—The Assignment 123

Afterword. 127
About the Author. 129

Acknowledgements

Thanks to Julius Lester, for inspiring the book, reading it, and believing in it; to Michael, for being the first to read it, filling the pages with constructive criticism, and creating a beautiful cover; to Tilman, for being a friend of almost forty years, who carefully read my book and through her own commitment to anti-racism work challenged me to look deeper into my own privilege issues; to Ted for walking miles in other people's shoes; and to Jane Lincoln Taylor, who edits with sensitivity and precision.

PREFACE

The Case for Diversity

SEVERAL years ago I began performing my one-woman play, *Not until You Know My Story*, as part of diversity trainings in corporations and government agencies. In the play I become fourteen "diverse" people, from an upper-class, bleeding-heart liberal (me) to an African American eighty-year-old sculptor and retired shoe repairman. The play is the catalyst for an audience discussion of prejudice and inclusion in the workplace. Usually people's walls of denial come tumbling down as audience members connect with the pain experienced by people on the receiving end of discrimination. However, after my first few trainings, an engineer at a technology firm wrote in his feedback that I needed to make the business case for diversity and how it relates to the bottom line. I conveniently compartmentalized his feedback, using my handy engineer stereotype to let me off the hook. "Come on, isn't it obvious? Of course it relates to the bottom line." I dismissed his comment as part of his denial and unwillingness to "go into his feelings" about the issue. The reality was that I had not realized the importance of making the case for diversity. I thought it was good enough to create and maintain a diverse workforce because it was the right thing to do.

Now I finally get what the engineer meant. Creating and maintaining a diverse workforce directly affects the success of an organization.

Any company, organization, or group cannot thrive when individuals have to leave part of themselves at the door. When employees experience events at work in which they feel hurt because of a prejudicial remark, if the environment is not set up to include everyone's perspective, the employees will make a survival decision: "I will not tell them what is true for me because they won't get it." They will leave that part of themselves, the part of them that was hurt, at the door. The employees will decide or be told that they are being too sensitive and that their focus should be on their work, not on a moment when they felt offended or not included. They will learn to desensitize themselves. They will turn off the parts of themselves that might get hurt or feel excluded.

The survival decision to leave part of myself at the door directly affects the bottom line. If I leave part of myself at the door, I will not have my whole self, my whole energy, available to solve problems creatively and contribute fully to the workplace. If people are making survival decisions based on "They won't get it," then they are constantly chopping off a part of themselves to fit in. The part they chop off might have been valuable to the company's ability to evaluate the work climate in which individuals thrive. It is crucial to find a way to connect with people who are perceived as different and who feel excluded, so they can bring their full selves to the workplace. A workplace with whole individuals has to be more productive than a workplace with people who need to use part of their energy to suppress their feelings and their experiences. Nell, a platinum-blonde software-company manager whom I portray in my play, states, in response to being ignored by a male colleague: "I felt completely excluded. It does something to you. It makes you feel like you aren't important. That you aren't making contributions. That they don't see you. Am I overreacting, is it me? Or is this guy a friggin' ignoramus?"

Full human beings make better employees, managers, presidents, partners, and (obviously) human beings. Human beings flourish when they are connected to who they are and to the people around them.

THE CASE FOR DIVERSITY

This is a book about making connections. The tool is simple: try to imagine how it feels to be someone who is different from you. The execution of the tool is the catch: "How can I imagine how it feels to be someone else when I am not that person?" Good question. You will never know how it feels to be someone else. That is where diversity starts. It also ends there unless you try to imagine how it feels to be the other person. The reason we are still talking about difference in the twenty-first century—as if it were a new concept—is that as a country and as individuals we are unwilling or afraid to try to imagine how it feels to be someone different from us.

The act of imagining how it feels takes energy and a willingness to feel uncomfortable. I have to be willing to struggle in the land of "I don't really know." The "I don't really know" land is a place we thought we were supposed to graduate from when we entered adulthood. Most of us adults do not want to go there. "Not knowing" is perceived as a state of weakness, yet whenever other people openly admit that they do not know, or when they share their struggles, I immediately feel my trust level increase.

Along with the willingness to feel uncomfortable, I also have to be willing to use some of my own pain as a door to walk through to imagine what you might be feeling. Although I have never been discriminated against on a continual basis because of my race, there have been moments in my life when someone has made a judgment about me that is not accurate. I feel enraged when a person decides that I am incapable of doing something I know I can do. Those moments in my life when I have felt the pain of being misjudged will allow me to begin to imagine some of the pain a person who experiences racial discrimination might feel.

Why in the world would anyone in a corporation want to expose employees to pain and discomfort? I have been asked that question quite a few times, usually by people who have the same skin color as I do and feel comfortably accepted in the workplace.

I can imagine asking the question. I feel accepted and liked at work. People smile at me if I begin to smile. They wish me a nice day without a second thought. Why should I mess with my own comfort? There is a cost to my comfort. I believe the price for my comfort is someone else's discomfort. As long as people respond positively to me just because of how I look, there will be other people who are responded to with suspicion and fear just because of how they look. Companies and government agencies hire me for diversity training because their white employees' comfort has become too expensive. High turnover is expensive. The workforce is continually becoming more diverse in race, gender, ethnicity, sexual orientation, disability, religion, and thinking style. We have to find a way to flourish from that diversity rather than hide from it by staying comfortable. When we reach outside our comfort zones we are in new territory. The struggle of trying something new and possibly uncomfortable opens the door to interaction and connection.

Diversity arises in the moments when we are not comfortable. I am challenged to grow by a person who has a different perspective. When we are in an unfamiliar place we feel less comfortable. Diversity is about the benefit that comes from making connections with people who are not familiar to us. If diversity and comfort were synonymous, then all diversity would require would be a few well-timed potluck dinners with ethnic dishes. If diversity were only a comfortable celebration of differences, then the work would be done and we would have a diverse group of people at the highest levels of our government and corporations. Everyone would be clamoring for more of that "fun diversity."

Diversity is not so easy as traveling to another country and enjoying the different people we meet. It is about trying to make a connection with a coworker or neighbor who pushes our buttons. Diversity is not just about race, gender, ethnicity, sexual orientation, class, disability, age, religion, size, or privilege. It is also about thinking style, job position, personality, and idiosyncrasies. It is in the moments when I do not want to be other people and I do not want to think like them or act like them that the challenge lies. It is in those moments also when the opportunity for growth and increased knowledge arises. The bottom line—

the productivity of a company and of any society—increases if we know how to respond.

Another person, also an engineer, came up to me after a training and said:

> Hey, I've really tried. I've been going to these trainings for three years now. I've really made an effort, you know, gotten to know people who are different from me. People come into my office and tell me what they're going through. I just don't know how much more time and energy I can put into this. It's hard. How do you know when we're done? What are we shooting for here? When is enough enough?

Fortunately, I did not tell him the short answer to his question: never. The goal of including a diverse group in all levels of an organization and working on our prejudiced beliefs is impossible to describe because we have not gotten there yet as a society. If I had an answer, then it would not be a truly diverse outcome; it would merely be my vision of the outcome. I do know that the goal is a journey. The journey begins when we are willing to confront our own hidden feelings and thoughts about prejudice and discrimination. Perhaps the outcome is the discovery of an exciting process that will never end. It is in not knowing the outcome that the adventure truly begins.

My journey and this book begin with who I am and how I arrived at the decision to confront the prejudiced beliefs with which I grew up. Julius Lester, my African American studies professor, introduced me to the idea of imagining how it feels to be people who are different from me. His invitation to try to imagine another person's reality forced me to look at my life and the issue of discrimination in a new way. My journey began with discovering the power of the tool he gave me. The tool of imagining how it feels to be someone who is different from me is what led to the creation of *Not until You Know My Story*. I wanted to force myself to imagine how it felt to be people who were not only different from me but also made me feel uncomfortable. In this book, you will meet some of the people I become in the play and many people I have met throughout the country as they make connections to others by trying to imagine the others' reality. This book will use their stories and my story to invite you to continue your journey with what may be a new tool, a way to cross a bridge to make connections with other people.

Before the adventure begins, I need to make a disclaimer. I have changed the names of the individuals in this book when they are mentioned in the context of trainings. The sharing that took place in the training sessions occurred with an agreement of confidentiality.

CHAPTER ONE

Where Did I Begin? Or, Why Me?

My mother came to visit me in Seattle from Washington, D.C. We were on a driving tour of the area where my husband and I wanted to buy a house. I loved the area because it was close to downtown and was one of the few parts of Seattle where the neighborhoods were ethnically diverse and community oriented. I showed her the playground where we often took our younger daughter. I proudly pointed out the line of children ready to jump on a swing that zipped down a cable. There was a group of children, from at least three different ethnic backgrounds that I could visually identify, playing soccer on the field next to the animal sculptures. I smiled as my mother let out an audible sigh that bordered on a moan. I knew her sigh was meant as a conversation opener, but I waited for a bit. Her second sigh was a full-fledged moan. My curiosity was piqued.

"What is it, Mom?" I asked, poised for one of "those talks."

She shifted slightly and asked, "This isn't the neighborhood where you are looking for a house, is it?"

I did not have a good feeling about this. I began to grip the wheel a bit harder. "Actually, it is. Why?" I asked, dreading the answer.

She leaned in as if I knew the secret. "The playground. It's awfully dark."

What I wanted to say was something with a hint of sarcasm thrown in: "What? The lighting is bad?" But I was frozen in anticipation and my creativity left me, so I urged her on. "What do you mean?"

She came right to the point. "The children are mostly black." Now I was starting to freak out inside. I tried to remain calm, thinking things such as, "Okay, I do diversity work, I can handle this." In order to clarify, she added: "I'm just thinking of Elsa."

I had a slight feeling of nausea as I tried to ignore my fear of where she was going with her concern for my daughter. "What's the problem?" I cringed slightly, trying to protect myself from the answer.

My mother had arrived at the place she was headed, the punchline. She had laid the groundwork. "If she becomes too comfortable with black children, she might marry one of them."

I was in total shock. The same fear she had found a multitude of ways to bring up to me as a teenager was now being transferred to my daughter. I flashed on arguments I used to have with both my parents about affirmative action, or the club we had belonged to, which allowed black people only to be workers, not members. My father listened while reading the newspaper. Eventually he would find a pause between my mother and me to squeeze in his intellectual analysis. "Carrie, it really boils down to economics. Socialist at twenty, you have a heart; at thirty you're a fool. You'll see." He would return to the business section of the *Washington Post*. At some point in the argument my mother's lip would begin to tremble and she would say, "Carrie, you can't marry a black man. Think of the life you would lead. Tell me you won't." I traditionally mumbled a variation of "I don't know what I'll do," but it took all my self-control not to say I was planning on marrying a black man as soon one became available, just to see her reaction.

Now here I was, twenty years later, in my car with my mother projecting her fear on my three-year-old daughter. My father was not part of these arguments anymore. When I was a teenager his alcoholism took hold, making him more invisible to my mother and me. He died in a nursing home from a brain disease caused by alcoholism before Elsa, our younger daughter, was born. His interjections never managed to take the emotion out of the arguments my mother and I had about racism. What would he have tried today? I was amazed that a simple tour of my future neighborhood had brought us to the same place our arguments used to bring us. I also irrationally became concerned about the possibility of other people discovering my mother's deeply rooted racism. I forgot we were in the car. What if someone overheard the conversation? What was I supposed to say to her?

I gasped slightly and managed to sum up the crux of her argument. "Marry one of them?" was the best I could do. I needed a moment to try to respond in a way that reflected that I had twenty more years of "maturity" in me. I realized I had better start to bring myself back to the conversation. "Mom, what are you saying? Elsa can marry anyone she wants. I don't care what color. And she is only three!"

My mother was not only ready to defend the fear she had had for me all these years, she wanted to bestow it on my daughter. After all, from her point of view, I had successfully married a white man, thanks to her influence. "Carrie, think of the children. Our family has not changed in generations. It's important to keep our family line pure. Our family line is very special."

At that moment I realized the reason behind her fear of interracial marriage. She had told me she was fearful of the pain an interracial family would have to experience in this society. She had couched her fear in her concern for her children's well-being. Now I realized that her fear had to do with the family line. If I had married a black man, I would have permanently ruined the calculated purity that gave my mother a sense of confidence and pride. The purity of skin color for my mother's family was intentional, and necessary to maintain what I perceived to be a sense of racial superiority.

A bit of background about my "family line":

My formal name is Diana Corona Gibson. My mother nicknamed me Carrie at birth; it was my parents' choice, following a family tradition: to give the children diplomatically chosen family names that my parents did not particularly like. The nicknames were what they would have formally named us if family tradition had not been such a strong force. My mother, Flo, has studied and documented her family tree to fifteen generations. Her stock is English, Scottish, and French, and, of course, white. It is a source of pride for my mother that "all of the slaves that were freed came back to [her] great-grandparents because the slaves were so kindly treated." My mother's family settled in Savannah, Georgia, and had a plantation where they owned slaves.

My mother married a white man, Victor Enrique Carlos Jose Gibson de Lira. (No, really, he was white. There were white Peruvians who came from Spain and darker-skinned Indian Peruvians who were conquered by them. My dad was definitely a white Peruvian.) His family came from Spain and England and had spent the previous six generations in Peru as part of the "aristocracy." My father was sent to England to be educated at the age of nine and was then transferred to the United States at the age of twenty because his father felt he was becoming "too English." He went to Harvard, where he met my mother through her brother. At the time of their marriage, my father made it clear that my mother was to stop her acting career because he was to be the breadwinner.

My mother sacrificed her acting career and, almost as if in exchange, my father traded in his Peruvian identity. Although he was still a Peruvian citizen, his white skin got even whiter. My mother called him Charles or Charlie at the country club. I did not find out I was half Peruvian until I was ten, when three loud women descended on my house to pinch my cheeks and gush things like: "Oooo, chiquicita, mi ninita." They acted different, they looked different, and they smelled different. They were my "tias"—not my aunts, but my "tias."

So there we all were, Washington D.C., 1962: my dad at the Peruvian Embassy and my mother with her finger on the pulse of the nation; charity work, cocktail parties, mingling with all the best Washington wives, including Jackie. Networking began at a young age for me; I was asked to join a playgroup with Caroline and John-John Kennedy.

WHERE DID I BEGIN? OR, WHY ME?

One day Jackie proposed that Caroline and John-John's playgroup become a school at the White House. I not only got to know Caroline and John-John, but I went to a school where during recess we might skip by the president on his break or climb over his desk in the Oval Office. During class we had to hold our ears because of those twenty-one-gun salutes with the big cannons. A typical field trip was a trip to an airfield so we could be among the first people to ride in a Goodyear blimp. We were given French lessons in kindergarten. I assumed it was all part of the standard kindergarten curriculum.

Until a few years ago, I was fairly adept at hiding the extraordinary privilege I had thought was just part of a normal childhood. My husband and I had been living together for a year before he knew where I had gone to kindergarten. We were visiting my parents in Washington, D.C. He came across the class picture with the White House in the background. "Honey, what's this?" he asked as he picked up the dreaded picture frame. I quietly mumbled, "Oh that's just a picture of me at the White House school." He leaned in a little closer to hear me. "What?" I knew I had been caught, so I boldly proclaimed, with an edge to my voice, "I went to kindergarten at the White House, okay? Can we just forget about it?"

Why did I feel naked when I confessed my kindergarten alma mater? I was scared that people would look at me differently. I was embarrassed by the amount of privilege I had taken for granted while growing up, and I did not want to be judged because of it. I found it hard to fight against social injustice while reeking of privilege. I am getting over my fear of disclosing my background. It is essential to own my privilege and where I come from so I can learn not to act on the prejudices with which I was brought up.

Meanwhile, back in kindergarten, there I was, one of the nice white kids in the nice White House. There was one "ethnic" child in our class, Avery Hatcher. He was a "Negro," the son of a Secret Service agent. I did not know anything about him except that I thought he was a prisoner of the White House because he was always there but he never made it to a single birthday party.

That was the beginning of my social activism. I began to question what other people seemed to take for granted. "Mom, how come Avery never comes to any of our birthday parties?" "Well, honey, he lives too far away." I do remember his father going to several birthday parties to guard Caroline and John-John, but Avery was not there. I never really got to know him. He seemed like a nice kid, but our contact was limited to classroom encounters. I wonder if he ever played with any of the other children.

After kindergarten at the White House school, we all went to Potomac Grade School, except Avery, of course, because he "lived too far away." Potomac School was a private school located in Virginia near the CIA headquarters. A lot of Robert Kennedy's children went there, along with children of various people who worked for the administration. It was a bit more racially integrated than the White House school. There were at least two African American children in each grade of forty children.

I made it to ninth grade somewhat oblivious that I had grown up in a city that was eighty percent African American. The only people I saw who were black were my friends' live-in maids (our maid was from Chile) and the allotted two black children per grade. My last year at Potomac, ninth grade, was the year we were to be educated about race. In a groundbreaking move, we, the white kids of Potomac School, were to meet black kids from the "inner city." We were each assigned a black student with whom to tour museums. We learned all about our black students. What did they do for fun? What did they eat? We were told to be their friends. At the end of two weeks, we stopped being their friends and sent them back to the "inner city." Our formal training in black people was complete.

During my school years, diversity had not become a valued goal to strive for. The focus of education was race relations. I never heard the term *diversity* until college. Integration was an issue involving black people and white people. All the other differences—ethnicity, gender, sexual orientation, disability, privilege, size, economic status—were rarely, if ever, mentioned.

I was now ready for high school. I was a teenager and my turn had come to find a way to rebel against my parents. I was the youngest of four, so all the good ways to rebel had been taken: sex, drugs, alcohol, running away, even suicide attempts. Because my siblings had already explored those avenues in depth, I needed to find an original form of rebellion. Then one day, I came upon the answer: the Chevy Chase Country Club, where the rich and Caucasian recreate. We were members. We were dropped off every weekend to play tennis and swim, and in the winter, to ice skate and bowl. We did not bowl with those big clunky bowling balls found in public alleys; we played duckpins with small balls. One day our club made the headlines of the *Washington Post*: "Mixed Doubles? Not Here. Chevy Chase bans Arthur Ashe."

From a young age, I had a developing sense of social justice. My mother was the only Democrat in her family of conservative Republicans, and we often argued politics with my father, who would definitely have been a conservative voter if he had become a U.S. citizen. He would always use an economic argument to justify wars or destructive policies. I became quite adept at finding the other humanitarian extreme, at which point my mother would intervene with a compromising middle that satisfied neither my father nor me. The banishment of Arthur Ashe because he was a black tennis player was the incident I was waiting for to assert my need to rebel.

I stormed into my parents' room and declared over their breakfast trays, "I vow, as long as I live, never to set foot in the Chevy Chase Country Club again."

My father straightened out a new section of newspaper while my mother looked up from hers. "Nonsense, dear, we all love the club."

I was not going to back down this time. It was time to make a stand. "Not me; there are no black people there."

My mother came right back with, "What about Robert and Cyrus? We all love Robert and Cyrus."

Okay, time to take out my big weapon: the M-word. "Mother." I paused. It worked. I got her attention. "Mother, they're waiters."

When I saw my mother's reaction, I knew I had made the right decision. I had successfully rebelled. A social activist was born. To my mother, not going to the club was much worse than one sister dropping acid or another sister totaling the family car while drunk. We never talked about those minor infractions. The family tragedy we still talk about is me not going to the club. Twenty-five years later, my mother still tries to end my "rebellion" by working on my husband or children to change my mind. She is still unsuccessful.

With my act of family rebellion and civil disobedience, I felt enlightened and ready to make a difference in the world. I went to Amherst College, a small, elite, private liberal arts college. Although Amherst was known as a hotbed of liberal thought, I encountered many people from privileged backgrounds similar to mine. I realized that my college choice was not exactly an act of civil disobedience. I needed to make a real statement, so I enrolled in a black studies course at the University of Massachusetts.

My decision arose from a lecture series that took place in Johnson Chapel. The chapel at Amherst doubled as an auditorium. The lecture series was about race and politics, in striking contrast to the walls of the chapel, which were lined with portraits of white men. I attended a panel discussion that included Julius Lester, a professor from the University of Massachusetts. He was an author and quite well known as a vocal advocate for civil rights in the sixties. I remember one moment when he pounded his fist on the table and addressed the sea of predominantly white faces in the audience: "You will never know how it feels to open your door on Halloween and have a nine-year-old girl jump back in fright because of the color of your skin. She thought I was wearing a costume meant to scare her. You will never know that hurt."

His intensity reached right into my stomach. I felt scared, and compelled to find out what he was talking about. The next day I enrolled in one of his courses; it was about W. E. B. Du Bois. I had never heard of Du Bois, a brilliant writer about injustice and humanity, but I was determined to take a course taught by Professor Lester.

Although I was nervous, there was also a part of me that felt quite pleased with myself. Here I was, a well-off, liberal white girl, going out of my way to learn about black people. I didn't have to. It was not even the 1960s. It was 1980. The class certainly wasn't going to help me toward my major. I enrolled in the course because I was a good person, and, who knows, as a late-adolescent rebel, I might get some more material.

I took my seat and glanced over at my new professor. Professor Lester was tall, and he wore a long wool sweater that opened in the front. I remember thinking how long his arms looked as he stood with his hands in the pockets of his well-worn sweater. He spoke in a deep voice as he introduced himself to the class. He took a seat behind the teacher's desk in the small classroom. I thought it was strange that this tall man sat behind a small desk. At Amherst College the teachers went out of their way to stand in front of the desks. Desks were frowned upon. The teachers lectured in front of the podium or sat with the students around a table, to create the illusion that they were like us. Nothing fancy here, just teachers and desks.

The semester began with us reading essays by W. E. B. Du Bois and discussing them in depth in class. Our writing assignments challenged us to begin to form our own values about life and justice. I remember an assignment in which we were each to write our own credo. I was forced to articulate my belief system for the first time in my life. Professor Lester challenged us over and over again to come out of our comfort zones and allow other people's experiences with racism or slavery to affect us. In the middle of the semester he had us read *Jubilee* by Margaret Walker, about Vyry, a woman who was a slave. I was horrified by the physical suffering inflicted on Vyry on a daily basis. I admired Vyry's courage and ability to keep her faith and sense of self, despite the violations she continually endured.

Professor Lester looked around the class of three white students and eight black students. (Another reason for me to feel proud of myself was that I had chosen to be in the minority.) We were discussing the emotional and physical pain Vyry had grown accustomed to in her life as a slave.

Professor Lester looked at the one white male student in the class and asked: "What do you think it would be like to be a slave?"

The young man froze for a moment, then shook his head. Finally, he answered: "I don't have any idea."

Professor Lester slammed the book he was holding onto the desk. He immediately got everyone's attention. "That's the whole reason there is suffering in the world. It's people's inability to imagine how it feels to be other people."

I remember the passion behind his words. I remember feeling ashamed that I had never really imagined how it felt to be the people about whom we had been reading. I felt as if he had exposed a part of me that had atrophied from lack of use. I realized that I had only skimmed the surface of the suffering we had been reading about because I was too lazy or too scared to put myself in the shoes of characters such as Vyry. To this day, Professor Lester is still getting my attention. Not every minute, not every day even, not so much as I might wish, but there are moments when his words totally hold me.

"Imagining how it feels to be other people" can get my attention for the rest of my life if I let it, and I want it to. The ability to imagine how it feels to be somebody else is the tool. We have all heard of it: "putting yourself in someone else's shoes." It is so simple, but we have yet to do it as individuals, as groups, or as a country. The national dialogue about diversity that occurs every day in the government or behind corporate walls, in my experience, rarely includes the practice of imagining how it feels to be people who still suffer the consequences of being perceived as different from the majority.

I know about it, I preach it in my trainings, I use it as an actor, but I still find a million reasons not to do it on a daily basis. When I head into a conflict or I meet someone who is so different from me that I feel uncomfortable, I rarely use my imagination to make a connection with what he or she might be thinking or feeling. Perhaps I have to write about it, just like writing a hundred times "I will try to imagine how it feels" on the blackboard. When I am finished, maybe then it will sink in.

Exercises:

- Imagine how it feels to be a slave. Write down whatever comes to you.
- Now imagine you are in a conversation with several people talking about their family lines but you can only trace your roots back to the name a slave owner gave your ancestor. How do you feel?

CHAPTER TWO

Exercising the Imagination

THE KEY to stopping suffering, in Professor Julius Lester's opinion (back in 1980), was to imagine how it feels to be somebody else. I was hooked. I wanted to end suffering. While my father focused on the economics of any situation, my mother taught me that it was my obligation to make a difference in the world. I took her teaching literally. "Ending suffering" was one of the most compelling causes I had heard of yet. I had to make things better. I came from a privileged, upper-class, white background and I had a social conscience. I had inherited and added to a bank of guilt born of my privilege, and I felt it was my job to end suffering. I sincerely wanted to learn how.

The next morning I headed off to UMass again, in search of Julius Lester's office. His door was slightly ajar and I peered inside, trying to see if he was hiding behind the stack of books on his desk. There were several African masks on his walls. The office was small and crammed with papers and books on the shelves surrounding his desk. For a moment I was absorbed in trying to read the titles of the books. I started slightly as I saw him leaning back in his chair, reading a student's paper. He had on a different sweater, a yellowing white sweater with black patterns outlining the bottom of it. The sweater was the same style I saw him wear in class; it opened in the front and had well-used pockets on the side.

I coughed lightly—my way of letting him know I was there. "Can I talk with you? I have an idea."

He immediately responded with his characteristic high-pitched laugh, and then said, "Uh-oh, not an idea. That could be dangerous."

I cleared my throat as he cleared a space for me to sit. I was slightly nervous to be with him one-on-one. I took the plunge. "I would like to do an independent-study course where all we do is imagine how it would feel to be people who are in suffering situations."

I waited. I realized that my words sounded slightly ridiculous. My face began to heat up. I blushed. Here I was, a well-off young white woman, asking this tall, slightly intimidating, and at times angry-sounding black man if I could get his help in imagining how it felt to suffer.

I sank a few feet into the hard chair. He let out a big laugh. That was it; I had to leave, and quickly. A minute of silence passed that felt like several hours of agony. I moved slightly in my chair, too scared to leave.

He finally spoke: "You must be slightly sick." See, I knew it, I was a fool. "You're definitely sick, but then again, so am I. I love it. Let's do it."

I began "Human Suffering 101," not having any idea what I was getting into. I had asked two friends to join me, both of them white. The reading list consisted of several books by Elie Wiesel, a Holocaust survivor, followed by a book or two on slavery and some we never got to. The first day Professor Lester asked the one question he would continue to ask the whole semester. "How do you imagine it feels to be this person or character?"

At first we responded to the question quickly, just trying to be right, as if being right were even relevant to the question. Professor Lester smiled and asked the question again. My comfort level went down a notch as I started to struggle for a different kind of answer. As he repeated the question, his words began to sound alien to me, as if he were speaking a different language. I resisted answering it by trying to give the intellectual response I had been taught at Amherst. "The situation is a difficult one in which...." My attempts at avoidance did not work with Professor Lester. Finally, the nature of the question forced me to search deeper and go to a place to which I had trained myself not to go. I had to enter the place inside myself where I hid my pain.

I had become expert at avoiding pain. I had been raised with comfort, not just in terms of my skin color and economic background, but in attitude. I did not have to suffer. I could change my circumstances. I could have anything I wanted if I wanted it badly enough. My family rarely showed emotions, and the "weak ones"—sadness, hurt, fear—were simply something to get over. I barely knew I was capable of feeling hurt or pain, much less violation and annihilation of spirit.

In my attempt to answer Professor Lester's question, I started to feel my own pain. Throughout the semester, as we tried to answer the same question, the response got easier and harder at the same time. The ease came because my imagination was getting exercise and becoming stronger. I was able to practice combining my imagination with my experience. We were developing a new muscle that we had never been taught to use before. It also became harder because we had to feel the pain each time we imagined how it felt to be one of the people in a situation of suffering.

I began to dream.

> I am sitting on a bus. I wear a scarf over my head. I want the scarf to protect me, to conceal my identity, but I know it is not enough. I feel intense fear and at the same time I try to prevent it from surfacing. The fear will make me more vulnerable; they can smell fear. I have escaped from a mental hospital where I have spent weeks pretending to be crazy. The oppressive environment of the hospital felt safer than the threat of being caught that waited for me on the outside. Now I am attempting to get to a ship that will take me to a place where I can be truly free and safe again.
>
> The bus approaches the docks. I can see the ship that will take me to a new home. Suddenly we stop. The squeak of the brakes increases the nauseated feeling in my stomach. The guards enter the bus, looking into each face. As they

approach, I desperately try to hide who I am, to hide my Jewishness. They go from row to row quickly; maybe they are not checking. A distant feeling of hope begins to flicker. I may be okay. One man looks at me, starts to move on, then stops. He comes back to me and talks in rapid German as he grabs my arm. I know I am going to die.

I woke up shivering and sweating at the same time. For the first time I let myself feel and explore my fear instead of resisting it. I realized that I had been given a gift, a chance to imagine how it might have felt to be a Jewish person in Europe during the Holocaust. I also knew that my dream came from my imagination, not from experience. I would never know or totally understand the real horror of the Holocaust, but my imagination, embodied in my dream, had invited me onto the bridge of connection.

I began to live with all the characters and people about whom we were reading. I felt I had to live with their suffering on a daily basis to imagine how it felt to be them. I spent hours talking with my two friends about the pain the people we read about experienced on a daily basis. I had convinced myself that the only way to connect with the people we read about was to feel the weight of their suffering in my body. I lost the spring in my walk and laughed less at people's jokes. I think I had taken the assignment a bit too far. Toward the end of the semester Julius (we had progressed from calling him "Professor" to "Julius") came in and looked at each of us for a moment before he spoke. "You all look awful." I felt awful. I was raw from trying to imagine how it felt to be all the people about whom we had read. We had all been mildly depressed for the past three weeks. "You need some medicine. Let's imagine how it feels to be in a world of pure joy. Read *The Last Unicorn*, by Peter S. Beagle. You are done with the suffering part of the course." I was relieved and yet slightly disturbed. How was I going to stop the suffering in the world if I didn't practice imagining how it felt all the time?

I took his advice and felt much better after a week of pure joy—so good that I did not really get back to the question "How do I imagine it feels to be that person?" for about eighteen years.

I heard his words in the back of my mind but was scared of the pain they had caused me to feel. Perhaps I needed to learn about my own pain before I could appreciate that his question had the power to energize me through human connection, rather than drain me through depression.

I chose to become a counselor because I thought I could continue to work on my goal of easing other people's pain. I entered the profession with the misguided belief that I had the power to cure other people of their pain. But my career choice did force me to break through the denial I had developed about my own pain over growing up in a family where alcoholism and manic depression played a significant role.

After I left college, I confronted my father's alcoholism through an intervention and family treatment. I decided that I needed to try to save all the other alcoholics in the world. In other words, my family issues made me a ripe candidate for the counseling profession. I might be able to learn enough to save my father and all the other alcoholics I could find. My mentors and teachers popped my "save the world" bubble and forced me to acknowledge my own pain and need for healing through therapy. Therapy is part of any good counselor's training. I discovered that by avoiding my own pain I had also avoided intimacy with other people. My denial of my own pain prevented me from connecting with other people. The depth of feeling I discovered in myself would also come in handy when I revisited the tool of imagination in my work and reentered the theater profession. I would need to have access to painful experiences in my life in order to imagine how it felt to be other people.

Sitting with people who are struggling with pain from their childhoods or their addiction problems could have been a perfect opportunity for me to practice imagining how it felt to be them. Unfortunately, I was so busy trying to "get it right" by following the latest counseling techniques that my imagination left the room.

There was so much emphasis on accurate listening that I rarely tried to put myself in other people's shoes. Instead, I tried to memorize their shoes, metaphorically speaking. I heard their words and could repeat them back perfectly, but I did not allow myself to connect with them. Listening skills are vital, but I now believe that without imagining how it feels to be other people while listening to them, the human connection is often lost.

Counseling was definitely not my ideal career choice. There was a deep passion inside me to be an actor and to let my imagination soar. I was unable to find my passion while sitting in a chair opposite a person who needed to do most of the talking in order to heal. I learned a lot from listening, but I found myself wanting to return to the theater and take the information and experiences I had absorbed into a role on stage.

My first premonition that counseling was not my ultimate destiny occurred during an intake interview with a client. I was working for an agency where my job was to spend two hours with each new client and find out everything I could about the client's experience of growing up in an alcoholic family. I had grown up in an alcoholic family and I was getting pretty familiar with certain similarities between my experience and that of the eighty or so people I had interviewed. In other words, I was starting to battle the urge to sleep in the midst of the interview. My husband had given me a "stay-awake" cup as a present. It had a funny face on one side and no face on the other. I looked at it through heavy eyelids as the woman opposite me described how she had felt when seeing her father drunk. I reached toward the windowsill, hoping to stay awake long enough to put my cup down. Suddenly I was wide awake, thanks to the crash my cup made as it hit the floor. I had missed the ledge by a good six inches. I blurted out something comforting like, "That sure got my attention," and stayed awake for the rest of the interview, thanks to an overwhelming sense of guilt.

I finally knew it was time to head back into theater and let my imagination back in the room on another day I will never forget. I was just starting to perform in a play about self-esteem I had cowritten for elementary schools. I felt an energy return to my life as I played the role of a ten-year-old girl in *The Best Possible Me*. I loved acting. I began to admit to myself that acting was in my blood. My mother was a successful actor who in her sixties created her own company to record classic books. Her second entry into theater culminated in her being nationally known as one of the best female narrators. I had a successful role model and no excuse not to try to make it as an actor. I reconnected with an energy and joy in my life through performing that I had never touched as a counselor.

The day I made the decision to change my career direction started out normally. I had several clients scheduled first thing in the morning. I was in private practice at the time with three other counselors who were all passionately devoted to their counseling careers. There was a performance of *The Best Possible Me* scheduled for my lunch hour, between clients. The night before, I had gotten a call from my agent about a movie audition for an early 1960s "barfly" type. I gathered all my outfits and arrived at the office in my counselor costume. After seeing two clients, I whipped into my barfly getup and rushed to the audition. I returned a barfly and dressed as a counselor again. After two more clients, I changed into a ten-year-old girl. I ran out of the office in pink high-top sneakers. I returned again a few hours later and got back into my counselor outfit. As I was changing clothes for the last time that day, I realized how natural it felt to keep changing costume. The problem was that if clients happened to see me in all the outfits I had worn that day, their confidence in me might wane a bit. They might think I was having identity trouble. The truth was, I had found my joy again, and it was not waiting for me in my therapy office. I realized I had been trying to save my family and the world through my profession, so I knew it was time for a change. I made a commitment to myself that day to devote my full time to my newly formed theater company, the G.A.P. (Growth and Prevention) Theater Company.

CHAPTER THREE

Fast Forward to Who Am I Really, and the Tool

I STEPPED out of my role as counselor and onto the stage in a theater company that focused on social-change issues. From age thirty-two to thirty-nine, I created and worked with the G.A.P. Theater Company. The first play we toured, to elementary schools, was *The Best Possible Me*. Schools loved hiring us to do a musical play about self-esteem. I built on the success of "growing" self-esteem and added a play the next year for middle-school children about feeling different. I wanted to help prevent the hurt caused by the many ways children can reject each other in late elementary through junior high school. Part of what fueled the topic of each play was my desire to educate my stepdaughter. I watched the issues she confronted as she approached her teenage years.

After three years of touring *The Best Possible Me, Do I Really Make a Difference?*, and *I'd Do Anything* (about environmental awareness), I decided it was time to revisit the issues of racism and discrimination. The idea immediately began to haunt me as I thought back to my "awakening" in college with Julius Lester. I somewhat guiltily realized that I had not really looked at the issue of racism since my independent-study course. In a way, the success and comfort I enjoyed in my twenties made it possible for me to ignore the issue of racism, because racism had no obvious negative impact on me.

I cowrote *The Hurt of One* with William Hill, an African American actor who was filled with talent and recent experiences of discrimination. We interviewed people from five different ethnic groups (African American, Latino, Native American, Asian American, and Euro-American) about their experiences in the United States and their knowledge of history that may have been left out of our textbooks. For instance, Robert Eaglestaff, a Native American school principal, told us about the smallpox-infested blankets that European settlers gave to the Native Americans. He explained how scalping was started by European settlers to prove they had killed "Indians." I left the interview in tears.

From the interviews and our own experiences of racism and privilege, William and I created a fictional play that took place in a school. We showed the subtle forms of racism that could occur in a classroom, in a faculty meeting, and between students. We cast five other actors from different ethnic groups to play multiple roles. We hired a composer to set poems to four-part a cappella harmony. The power of music coupled with the raw emotion from each actor's personal experiences created a play that took on a life of its own. *The Hurt of One* became the G.A.P. Theater Company's most popular and controversial play. We were all catapulted into an intense schedule of performing a play on racism and then riding together in a van where we had to deal with our own realities of either experiencing or unconsciously perpetuating racism.

There I was, traveling with six other actors from five different ethnic groups (I was the only "white girl" again). I spent seven years creating and touring plays to schools with the mission of eradicating racism, sexism, pollution, and low self-esteem. It was a tough job, but I still thought I could do it.

While traveling from school to school, various actors had epiphanies about their own experiences of racism or discrimination. I watched people I thought I knew pretty well suddenly lose their protective shell as they started to cry in the van on the way home from a play. I, being the "together" one (the founder, and white), listened and occasionally got to hug them. They all knew a little about my family, but I never talked about what it was like to eat, drink, and breathe privilege on a daily basis. I did not tell them I had been trained to believe I was better than they were. I did not tell them that I had gone to kindergarten at the White House with Caroline and John-John. I did not tell them that I still responded from my prejudices. I was too ashamed to tell them the truth; I wanted them to like me.

I was one of two white people in a cast of seven actors. The other white person was a gay white man who often spoke of the discrimination he experienced because of his sexual orientation. Although the other actors were not aware of the economic privilege I had grown up with, the experiences we each had in our travels pointed to the many privileges I had taken for granted as a white woman. I began to recognize my privilege in contrast to the experiences of the actors of color.

I define privilege as the benefits I automatically receive because of my skin color. The list of privileges I have learned to recognize continues to grow each day. When I refer to privilege throughout this book, it encompasses one or more of the following:

- I have the privilege of being able to trace my family line as far back as I choose to. People who have ancestors who were brought here as slaves do not.

- I have the privilege of expecting fair treatment in a public place. For instance, I expect to be served in a restaurant when it is my turn. When I went to restaurants with the cast members from G.A.P. who were not white, we were often served last even if we ordered before other people.

- I have the privilege of walking out of a store holding items without a shopping bag or receipt and receiving a smile from the salesperson rather than an accusation from a security guard or store manager.

- I have the privilege of being greeted with warmth rather than suspicion by salespeople when I enter a store.

- I have the privilege of being smiled at without fear and suspicion by people I see on the street.

- I have the privilege of being trusted without showing an I.D. all the time.

- I have the privilege of having been educated by teachers who had high expectations of my work and my future.

- I have the privilege of completely trusting that the police are here to protect me rather than pull me over as a possible suspect because I "fit the description." (William was repeatedly pulled over by police on the way to our performances. His license tags were up to date and he was not speeding.)

- I have the privilege of seeing people who share my skin color portrayed positively in the media.

- I have the privilege of seeing many people who look like me in positions of power.

- I have the privilege of believing that if I work hard enough for something I will probably get it.

- I have the privilege of expecting fair treatment.

- I have the privilege of living almost anywhere I want without fear of being ostracized by the community or the fear of having to go to extraordinary lengths to get a mortgage.

- I have the privilege of feeling people relax when they see me, as opposed to the subtle fear response African American men learn to expect.

- I have the privilege of being able to relate to discrimination because I am a woman, but still expect to have a certain amount of influence and power because I am white.

- I have the privilege of feeling, in a majority of situations and with most groups of people, that I belong.

- I have the privilege of receiving more eye contact from hotel clerks, salespeople, and restaurant employees than nonwhite people do.

- I have the privilege of succeeding in a system that was created by and in many ways is still controlled by white people.

- I have the privilege of denying that I benefit from racism because I benefit from racism every day.

- I have the privilege of "seeing no color or visual difference" because I am not negatively affected by my skin color most of the time.

- I have the privilege of not working on my own prejudices because of all the privileges I have listed here.

I have listed privileges that I am able consciously to identify. I wrote this list before reading an article by Peggy McIntosh, "White Privilege and Male Privilege,"[1] in which she lists forty-six privileges she receives because she is white. Although traveling with G.A.P. actors allowed me to discover privileges I had taken for granted most of my life, I did not take the risk of sharing a lot of them out loud with my fellow cast members. I was too heavily invested in trying to fit in and feel included. Fortunately, I did not totally get away with hiding my privilege. There were moments in the G.AP. van when people would get in touch with their anger toward the power structure. In those moments I was unable to hide my identity, a white woman in the power position of being the director of the company.

Sharon was a wonderful actor and someone who, I felt, was becoming a good friend. She was Japanese American. One day as the van pulled into the park-and-ride she asked if everyone could stay for a few minutes. We all agreed. She looked nervous as she began to speak:

---

[1] Peggy McIntosh, "White Privilege and Male Privilege," Working Paper no. 189 (Wellesley, Mass.: Wellesley College Center for Research on Women, 1988).

I am having trouble with you being in charge and being white. Everything you do comes from your privilege. If we can't find a parking place, you go out and ask someone to move up. I would never do that. You are so different from me. When I try to challenge you on a decision, you always give me a reason. You, as a white person, have the privilege of being defensive. As a person of color I don't even have that right. My defenses have been taken away.

My biggest fear was coming true. I felt a pit inside my stomach as I tried to brace myself for what I knew was coming. She reached for another actor's hand. All eyes were on her. I looked calm but on the inside I was screaming with terror. I was used to being right, and being everyone's friend. I had grown accustomed to feeling that I belonged in any group, even the diverse group of actors I had hired. Suddenly, Sharon had turned what I had come to expect upside down. I felt as if she were declaring that my privilege excluded me from ever belonging in their group. Ironically, the hand she was holding belonged to the one white male in the group. I wanted him to be my ally, but even he was in their club because he was a gay white male battling discrimination.

Sharon started to cry as her voice increased in volume with the anger she was feeling. A few of the actors moved closer to her to support her in her feelings. I tried as hard as I could to hear her without defending myself. I knew that I had to respond the right way or I would be attacked by everyone. Unconsciously, I probably feared that I would lose my power and control. In a slightly paranoid way, I was just waiting for all of them to say they hated me and that I was a fake.

If there was ever a time not to be defensive, this was it. What was that tool I had talked about after the play with the high school students? I was supposed to imagine how it felt to be her. My fear took over and I went blank. I tried to hear her pain and respond with "I hear your pain *and*. . . ." I thought "and" sounded so much more open than the defensive "but." "I hear your pain *and* I need to tell you what is going on with me." I thought I was being so open, and then *wham!* More anger was coming at me.

My speaking was like using lighter fluid to put out a fire. I even responded with silence but that didn't work either. Inside I was feeling hurt, too, but I knew no one wanted to hear about my feelings. I also felt that no one really saw me for who I was. The truth was, no one really knew who I was because I was too scared of being judged for it.

I started to feel the pain that I had felt growing up in my dysfunctional family. The alcoholism and manic depression in my parents and siblings left me feeling different, and in a strange way excluded. "They see me but they don't really know me. They hear me but I can't really tell them how I feel. I feel so visible and yet totally invisible at the same time." I had no idea that what I was feeling would give me a door to walk through to imagine how it felt to be someone whom I perceived as "different" on a daily basis. From that day on in the theater company, I felt totally alone. I lost the connection I had been starting to build with the other people in the group. I hid my feelings and who I was from them, and from myself, more than ever. If only I had responded with "Can I try to imagine how you feel when I always have a reason?" I could have tried to walk across the bridge of connection. I was not ready, and too scared, to risk feeling my pain, let alone try to imagine Sharon's pain or the obstacles she faced daily. The lack of connection grew into the beginnings of burnout in me.

The final four years of G.A.P. were my crash course in witnessing the personal pain that discrimination brought to an individual. I saw blatant forms of racism: a student would stand in front of five hundred other students and say, "Why don't you people go back where you came from? Go back to Africa." I listened to the rage and pain expressed by William and Edmonia, company members who had thought, as I had, that such blatant racism did not exist anymore. I also felt some of the pain caused by the subtler forms of discrimination. For instance, school employees would tell us that they had shortened our program by half because there just was not enough time to "do everything." The idea of "doing diversity" in forty-five minutes was not only absurd but an effective way to prevent any substantive changes in racist practices from occurring. I had witnessed the moment when Richard, another company member, saw his denial of the effects of racism on his own life come crashing down. He had internalized the stereotypes he was raised with about Native Americans and on some level wanted to be white: "I look in the mirror and I see a white person because it would be just too bad if I really saw the Indian."

I had learned much about the reality of being a person of color in a country where being white is for the most part an advantage in achieving success. However, the last confrontation with Sharon left me feeling alone; I was not ready to own the depth of privilege I received because of my skin color. I did not try to imagine how it felt to be her that day; I felt I had to defend myself and my position. The lack of connection I felt with the other actors could have been resolved if I had taken the risk of doing my own work on understanding and confronting my privilege. After the confrontation, for the first time I began to feel emotionally drained instead of filled with insight and energy after traveling with the company. Several months later I came to the conclusion that staying much longer in the company would take a severe toll on my physical and spiritual health. I resigned from my role as actor, director, and board member. The lack of connection I felt led to my sense that the only option was to leave. I was also ready for a change after ten years of wearing as many hats as I could find to keep G.A.P., a nonprofit, afloat.

Why do organizations have a hard time retaining employees who are perceived as different? I had firsthand experience. I lost the feeling of connection with the other actors. I was like the employees who have to go to work but leave a part of themselves at the door because other people do not take the time to make a real connection with them. In this case I was the one who did not reach across and with my imagination try to make an emotional connection with Sharon. I was disconnected and eventually felt the need to leave. Connection is vital to the bottom line. Without connection, people make self-preservation decisions, just as I did. I resigned.

The ironic part was that I had talked, in the debriefings after our performances, about the tool of imagination and its role in creating connection. I was quite articulate about the power of imagining how it felt to experience feeling invisible and totally visible at the same time because of skin color or size or accent or whatever. I pleaded with high school students to imagine how it felt to be the person toward whom they felt violent. Back in the G.A.P. van, when Sharon confronted me with the idea that, by definition, being white in a power position meant that some of my actions or statements would be informed by racist beliefs, even if those beliefs were held unconsciously, I went blank. Sharon gave me the chance to look at my own racism. The definition of racism I use is "prejudice backed up by institutional power." My actions in the company were backed up by power. I had grown up believing that it was my right to defend myself, and she had grown up feeling the need to give up all defenses in order to fit in.

Privilege also played a significant role in my decision to resign. I knew I could move on and either find or create a new job for myself. The only obstacle I would have to face was insecurity about my ability to succeed. Sharon and the other actors of color in G.A.P. did not have the same kind of choice. They, of course, could choose to leave, but they would face other obstacles in addition to the lack of self-confidence. There was, and still is, a significant difference in the number of roles available to actors who are not white. My decision was facilitated by skin-color privilege.

As I began to identify the active role privilege and racism played in my life, I began to grapple with the corresponding responsibility that goes with privilege. I could have left G.A.P. in the hands of someone just like me, a white woman who tried to "do it all." Fortunately, the ethnically diverse board of directors and my own commitment to diversity made that choice feel almost impossible. I made a conscious effort to reach out to candidates who not only did not consider their experience a match with the job of a managing artistic director but also were very different from me. We found people who had worked for G.A.P.

as actors and interviewed them, knowing they could learn the position. G.A.P.'s leadership in the following years was made up not only of people of color, but also of people who challenged the system that I had created. At times the road was rough, but in the long run the company reinvented itself with a new vision generated by different perspectives.

Turning forty marked the beginning of a new kind of freedom for me. It took forty years for me to realize that I really was who I was, a woman who grew up with skin color and economic privilege, and it was a form of dishonesty to hide it. After leaving G.A.P., I came out of the closet with my privilege, using the vehicle of theater and a one-woman play. If I was going to come out and say who I was, I might as well tell several hundred people at a time. Unfortunately I had to walk through the desert of transition to arrive at my new career choice.

I left G.A.P. and began trying to find a career that would fill the hole left by the energy and constant attention it had taken to create and run my own theater company. In an attempt to avoid the angst of "not knowing," I considered the option of abandoning the theater entirely and getting a job in diversity at a major corporation. My husband and friends intervened and encouraged me to persevere through the hard times of trying to make a living as an actor. At one point I went to a psychic counselor and asked her what I was supposed to do with my life. She looked at me and said, "You need to create something new. Do not try to fill your time with a job that already exists. Go into a theater and stare at an empty stage until you invent a new form for yourself."

I thought she was totally wrong. I tried to ignore her advice completely. I spent the year after G.A.P. vowing on a daily basis that I would pursue acting without any agenda. I decided to join the movement of bliss followers and pursue theater purely for the love of theater. I released myself from having to be a change agent. I resigned again from the job of trying to eliminate suffering through getting people to imagine how it felt to be other people. I tried to lay down for a second time the tool of connection Julius Lester had taught me.

Then my husband and I went to the theater to see Anna Deveare Smith perform *Fires in the Mirror*. She had interviewed people following the riots in Los Angeles and, using their words, put together a series of monologues in which she became them fully. I fell completely in love with the idea of being real people. The psychic was right, except that the stage I saw was not empty. Anna Deavere Smith brought real people to life on stage. I wanted to do that and incorporate them into my own experience of privilege and prejudice. I began to interview people whom I had met through the seven years of touring with G.A.P., and people whom I have known all my life.

I had no idea I was creating a theater piece that would force me to pick up where I had left off in my "Human Suffering" class. I did not know that I was ready, not just to teach high school students the technique of imagining how it feels to be other people, but to practice it. I do not know why I had no idea. One would think I would have realized that to be a good actor I had to imagine how it felt to be other people. I also did not realize that the tool was essential to, and often missing from, the dialogue about diversity.

I began each interview by asking, "What is it like to be you?" The answer usually lasted a full hour, with only a few prompting questions from me. I approached each interview the way I thought an actor would: totally unattached to whether I agreed with or even liked what the person said. I wanted to put myself in others' shoes, so the questions that kept floating in my head were: "I wonder what he is feeling right now?" or "How would I feel if what she is describing happened to me on a daily basis?" At times I felt tears well up in my eyes. I felt twinges of rage and anger. The one thing I did not feel in those sacred hours with people, who shared their pain and their lives with me, was judgmental about their points of view. The absence of judgment allowed the people I interviewed to feel safe enough to tell me what they really thought and felt.

People connected with me because, in order to try to imagine how it felt to be them, I had to leave my judgments and my defenses out of the room. The tool allowed me to take a vacation from my defenses and judgments, which resulted in truly effective and productive communication. I felt I had discovered the missing link in the conversation about diversity that has been going on since the early 1970s.

One of the people I interviewed was my mother. She and I had become accustomed to discussions about racism and heterosexism and any kind of "-ism," in which we would both tenaciously hold onto our points of view. I asked her about her family's experience with race in this country. I wanted to know how she had arrived at her current views of racism and the origins of her fear of interracial marriage. Several times, as she began to talk freely, she would stop midsentence and say, "You won't like this but. . . ." I would immediately interrupt her and assure her that I wanted to learn about her, not impose my opinions. I was amazed to see her begin to open up and tell me parts of her family's history that I had previously been too scared and judgmental to find out about.

> My father came from Georgia, and, by the way, during the Civil War, his grandparents—all of the slaves that were freed came back because they'd been so kindly treated. I mean it was a very, very kind atmosphere. And they loved dearly the people that worked for them, but I think my father was brought up at a time where there were very few educated blacks around and he did not realize that the black people were getting the education they are today. And that's, that's what it really boils down to in many ways. How capable and competent and educated a person is. . . . My father had a mammy who he loved dearly, who sang him to sleep every night, and he absolutely worshipped her. But she was there as his nurse. That was understood.

I remember going up to the room I had occupied as a teenager, where my husband was relaxing with a book. He asked me how the interview went, and judgment suddenly came flooding into my brain. I said to him, "Well, that was a waste of time. Just more of the same old stuff I was raised with. I don't think I got anything usable."

A month later I actually listened to the tape and realized that not only did I have some good material for the play, but the character of my mother would be one of my biggest acting challenges. I had to imagine how it felt to be her instead of evaluating her perspective in relation to mine.

I asked John Vreeke, a wonderful director and adapter of plays, to help me take the material from the interviews and create a play. The writing process continued right through the first three months of performance. The response of audience members often resulted in rewrites and occasionally in the addition of a new voice. The most personally challenging addition was the need for me to interview myself. After John had watched the play for a few months, he said, "You seem smug. Something's missing." He was right. I needed to interview myself and expose my own vulnerability, pain, and prejudices. Finally, nine months after my first interview, John and I knew we had a powerful play.

We titled the play *Not until You Know My Story*; the alternate title was *A Fly in the Buttermilk*. Both titles came from the words of people I had interviewed. The phrase "not until you know my story" came from an interview with Norm Stamper, who was the chief of police of Seattle. He said, "Not until I know the stories, not until I know the kind of suffering that that person has experienced, not until I know the path that you have traveled, can we be truly unified."

He had spent years thinking about the importance of creating a workplace that was safe and engaging for all kinds of people. He truly believed that a way to develop connections with people was to learn their stories. He also impressed me as one of the few people I have met who consistently imagine how it feels to be other people. He captured the importance of imagining how it feels to be another person in the phrase "not until. . . ." Not until I know my coworkers' stories, whether the stories of their lives or of what happened to them on the way to work, will I be able to stop making assumptions. In order to connect, to try to imagine how it feels to be someone else, I would have to listen to his or her story.

The phrase "a fly in the buttermilk" came from Edmonia Jarrett. Edmonia had retired from the school system to devote her time to performing in the theater and singing jazz. I met her at the auditions for *The Hurt of One*. Not only did I know she was right for the part in the play, but my family and I grew so close to her that she became our younger daughter's surrogate grandmother. In her interview she said:

> I worked in the school system for twenty-five years. I was a teacher, an administrator, a principal, and a doormat. Being a black woman, the good ol' boys didn't hold the same conversations. My mother used to say to me, "Honey, it's like you're the fly in the buttermilk and you are paddling like hell and everybody else got a raft." To know that you're alone.

I began to take *Not until You Know My Story* into corporations and communities as a vehicle to model the tool of connection—imagining how it feels. I began to apply the tool to people's comments after the play. I watched as whole groups of people struggled to imagine how it felt to be a woman who felt invisible to her male colleagues, or a black man who during the workweek was everyone's buddy and then on the weekends was not recognized by his coworkers. An amazing thing was happening before my eyes. As people tried to imagine how it felt to be the person who brought up an issue, that individual and the group as a whole became more engaged. I might see the person who bravely broke the ice and talked about her hurt nod her head, lean forward, tear up, or simply become more energetic. I watched the other people in the audience do the same as they tried to put themselves in the situation their coworker had described. I saw people connect with and deepen their trust of each other.

In my G.A.P. years, I had seen postplay discussions in which people who spoke about painful situations shut down because their coworkers did not know how to "get it." Instead of imagining how it felt, people would respond in the following ways:

- Silence; no one would respond to the comment. After a full minute or more of silence, another audience member would raise a hand and say, "I have something I want to bring up," and successfully change the subject to a "less threatening" issue.

- Laughter, either a self-deprecating joke made by the speaker to take the pressure off the room or a joke someone else made. The laughter had a cleansing effect that let people off the hook.

- "Yeah, that happened to me and this is how I have learned to deal with it." Somebody else would share his or her pain. The intention of sharing the pain may have been to connect, but the result would feel more like: "Enough about your pain; let's talk about my pain."

- "This is not the appropriate forum for that issue. Let's take it off line." Or, "We just don't have time to get into that right now." Every work culture or group has its own way of saying, "Do not talk about that here."

This list could go on. People simply have not been given an effective way to respond when a person brings up painful issues. Every one of those examples takes away the chance to address an issue that could increase not only the inclusivity of a work group, but the productivity and personal relationships in that group. By not connecting with the person, the message the group gives is "It's not safe to talk about those things here." People are forced to leave part of themselves at the door. A decision to survive in this group emotionally by leaving the "sensitive" part of me at the door results in my being numb to what is not working. A vital source of human feedback about the healthy functioning of a work group is eliminated.

As noted above, a company, organization, or group cannot thrive when individuals have to leave part of themselves at the door. If I leave part of myself at the door, I will not have my whole self, my whole energy, available to solve problems creatively. I also will not trust or connect with my coworkers. If I am not able to communicate openly with and trust my coworkers, the work environment becomes vulnerable to unspoken resentments and possible hidden hostility. Without a mechanism to incorporate feedback and conflict openly, I experienced a lack of trust and connection with the members of G.A.P. The energy that emanates from an open, trusting environment was transformed into negative, draining energy. I made a self-preservation decision, not unlike one that would be made by a person who is perceived as different and "too sensitive" in any workplace. The lack of connection was one of the reasons I quit.

The tool, imagining how it feels to be another person, provides a constructive communication path that leads to a powerful result. The result is connection, the antidote to having to make a self-preservation survival decision. The rest of this book will illustrate the power of the tool with examples that have come up in my years of practicing it around the country. Before I illustrate the effectiveness of the tool, I need to say what it is not.

The tool or technique is not the answer; it is not even *an* answer. It is a process, a different kind of questioning and seeing. The result of the process is unknown but always surprising and beneficial.

"I imagine you might be feeling..." is not related to the statement "I know how you feel." "I know how you feel" leads the list of ineffective communication statements. The truth is I will never, ever know how it feels to be someone different from me. I believe, though, that if I do not try to imagine how it feels, the dialogue about diversity will never lead to meaningful action. We have to find the bridge, a place where we can meet and connect, to move forward and truly embrace our richest commodity: *all* people.

The tool is not a cure for my prejudices. I toured the play for three months before John, my director, confronted me about my smugness. He had caught me. I did think I had it all together. I had a tool that cured me of the prejudices I was raised with in this country and in my family, right? Wrong! My prejudices, my feelings of superiority to other people, still exist. The tool simply allows me to prevent my prejudices from influencing my actions and statements when I am using it. When I listen to people and I focus on trying to imagine how it feels to be them, I am not listening to the part of my mind that still plays old messages about people different from me. Instead I feel an openness to their experience and perceptions.

Using the tool is not always easy. If I can immediately say, "Oh, I can imagine how it feels to be him, he enjoys irritating me," I am wrong. I cannot cheat and simply endow other people with my own assumptions about them. Few people wake up and say to themselves, "Hmm, today I think I feel like being particularly irritating to others." If I really apply my imagination, I might discover a mix of fear and insecurity behind the source of my irritation. To imagine how it feels to be another person, especially a person who is irritating me, requires thought and vulnerability on my part. I have to be willing to let go of my irritation in order to imagine the other person's feelings. The feelings I imagine may awaken painful memories for me. When I let myself have access to those feelings, the irritation and judgment are transformed into human connection.

The technique of imagining how it feels to be the other person seems relatively simple on the surface. The tool has the power to transform irritation into human connection. Now it is just a matter of putting it into practice. No problem, right?

Exercises:

- List all the privileges you take for granted just because of your gender, your skin color, and/or your age.
- List the ways you or other people have responded to someone when he or she confronts a behavior or statement that hurts them. How do you imagine it feels to be that person?

CHAPTER FOUR

No Problem Here

As A COUNTRY we have not yet fully embraced the concept of diversity. People who are not white and male are for the most part underrepresented in the media, the political power structures, corporations, and educational institutions in the United States. Institutional power is mostly in the hands of people who are white and male. The 2000 election contest between Al Gore and George Bush made history partly because there was not a large contrast between two white men with centrist views who both have risen to positions of power with relative ease. The people of this country had a hard time making a choice. Every time the newspaper showed a picture of the two major candidates, the word "diversity" did not jump off the page.

People often question the assumption that diversity has not been fully embraced. I frequently hear the question: "Is there really a problem with diversity, or are we just making it a problem by talking about it?" A related question is "Is there any value in diversity?" These questions provide a great opportunity to apply the tool of trying to imagine how it feels to be someone with a different perspective.

I have been asked those questions in a wide variety of settings. In a small town in the eastern part of Washington State, a student asked: "Aren't you creating a problem by talking about diversity? We don't have any problems with it here."

I imagined what the person who asked the question was feeling and how he had developed that perspective. The community for which the G.A.P. Theater Company was performing was not diverse in terms of race and ethnicity; there was not one person of color in the audience. Because I was one of two white people in the cast, I did not experience any problem with feeling included at the school either. People seemed friendly and open in their interactions with me. My experience was completely different from that of William, an African American actor, who walked down the hall to go to the bathroom and heard several students say hurtful slurs under their breath. From the student's perspective there really was no reason to talk about an issue that did not exist for him.

Now I am imagining reading that last paragraph and thinking how obvious it is that in a small community that is predominantly white, people would not want to address diversity actively. I was conducting a training in the Bay Area for a company that was not only diverse but prided itself on doing in-depth diversity training. A woman raised her hand to get my attention during a workshop after seeing *Not until You Know My Story*. She said, "I don't see people's color or their differences. I think we are all the same. Why do we have to talk about it at all?"

Her face reddened with emotion as she addressed the question to her colleagues and me. She appeared to be passionate and adamant in her belief that we were all the same. Again, I imagined that her passion was backed up by her experience. She treated people fairly and more often than not experienced similar treatment from others. She probably had never experienced being followed in a department store by a security guard because of her skin color. From her perspective there was no problem with diversity in her life. She felt included and welcomed in most of the interactions she had with other people.

In the previous two examples, the question of whether diversity needed to be addressed as an issue came up in completely different settings. There is sufficient evidence for me to realize that the concept of diversity is not welcomed automatically anywhere, no matter how liberal or conservative, how rural or urban, how big or small, or how homogeneous or diverse. I am still surprised when the controversy appears in my own backyard. Just this morning I was struck by Dorothy's wisdom in *The Wizard of Oz*. She said to Glinda, the Good Witch of the North, "If I can't find it in my own backyard, then I never lost it in the first place." In terms of diversity, I would rewrite that statement to say, "If I can't struggle with diversity in my own backyard, then I'll never find it in the first place." In other words, diversity is controversial everywhere, including my own backyard. Why would I think my backyard is the only place in this country where prejudice and exclusion do not exist?

My younger daughter attends an independent private school where social and environmental issues are integrated into the curriculum. The school prides itself on having an antibias curriculum and a student body more diverse than those of most of the other schools in the area. A friend of mine and I formed a diversity committee to support the antibias work that was supposedly already in place. Why was I surprised to find out that simply forming a diversity committee would be controversial? Suddenly we were in the middle of a controversy in which there were parents saying, "We are of one race, the human race. Why do we need to make a problem out of something that is already working?"

Apparently the universe needed to make certain that I understood that diversity is an issue everywhere, and especially in my own backyard, because that is where I have to do my own work. The universe also provided me with a concrete illustration of the power of crossing the bridge to connect with people who have different perspectives. In my last two examples, I made an effort to imagine where the people who did not want to address diversity were coming from. Now I want to invite people from that perspective to cross the bridge to connect with people who believe in the value of diversity and of addressing the issue of bias. Most of us human beings do not want to make a problem out of something that seems to be working for us. That sentiment is not only understandable but completely logical.

A concerned father who wanted to make sure the diversity committee at my daughter's school did not create problems said to me: "Why do you make it your battle to fight skin-color prejudice or to get more access for people with disabilities? Isn't that their battle to fight?"

What a great question. He challenged me to justify why I have spent the last ten years of my work life using theater to address issues of prejudice and discrimination. After giving his question some serious thought, I told him that if the people who still hold the most power and influence in this country because of their skin color do not join with people who feel disenfranchised, the battles will never be won. We can refuse to change or be willing to join in the battle for change. If the concerned father were to imagine how it felt to be excluded because of difference, I believe he would want to be part of the effort to open up more opportunities for people who have been discriminated against.

The perspective I want to invite you and the concerned father to imagine is the perspective of someone who is experiencing ongoing or even occasional problems because of a difference in skin color, ethnicity, size, race, economic background, religion, ability, disability, or sexual orientation. (Please add to the list any difference that I have left out.)

The challenge here is to put aside your opinion for a moment. I challenge you to cross the bridge, even if your perspective is the complete opposite of mine. Join me in my imagination as I cross the bridge to try to connect with parents in the schools my children have attended.

- I imagine the rage I would feel as an African American parent who had to explain to her child why the maps still used in most classrooms showed Africa as fourteen percent smaller than it actually is.

- I imagine the sadness and pain I would feel as I explained to my child why some of the kids told him he could not be Harry Potter in the school play because he is black.

- I imagine feeling the pain and injustice of having to explain why a picture in a history book might be altered to make the man who was a great explorer in his time appear to be white, not black.

- As my child grew older, I imagine the sadness I would feel having to educate him about how to respond to being pulled over by the police or security guards simply because he looked different from other people.

- I imagine the pain I would feel if I were a lesbian parent and my child came home from school crying because people had laughed when the teacher tried to explain what a homosexual was when talking about the people Hitler tried to annihilate.

The following imaginings come from characters I portray in *Not until You Know My Story*. Each of them told me what he or she experienced because of being perceived as different in this country.

- I imagine the fear, anger, and confusion I would feel if a child came up to me and said, "You people come from monkeys and that's the reason you can't think and that's how come you're not smart." Fear because the year was 1997 in the Northwest, and I had hoped I would leave extreme prejudice where I grew up, in the 1940s in the South, when the water fountains still had signs saying "For whites only."

- I imagine the degradation and self-hatred I would feel if, as a Native American child, I was told by my adoptive mother, "Come up to the top of the steps to get your food, take it downstairs to eat it, and bring the dirty dishes to the top of the stairs," because I was the "Indian boy who lived in the basement."

- I imagine the rage I would feel as an adult when a police officer pulled me away from my meal in a restaurant because I "fit the description" of an "Indian."

- I imagine the shock and pained indignation I would feel if my boss continued to address my work group of four managers using the term "gentlemen" when I was the only woman.

- I imagine the grinding anger and exhaustion I would feel if had to do every job twice as well as my coworkers because I was African American.
- I imagine the hurt and anger I would feel if my colleagues did not use my computer program because I spoke with an accent.
- I imagine the confusion and anger I would feel if I were not paid the same rate as my coworkers because I was a Chinese American who spoke with an accent.
- I imagine the pain and sadness I would feel if people pretended I was invisible when they dropped off their children at school because I was a teacher's aide who happened to be Latina.
- I imagine the rage and sorrow I would feel every time I heard of another suicide by a teenager who was ostracized by his peers or family because he said he was gay. The rage would be tinged with deep sadness because I had to be almost forty years old to have the courage to tell my parents I was gay.

It is hard to imagine denying the importance of addressing diversity when I listen to each of those stories and try to connect with them. I will never know what it is like for each of these individuals, but I can use moments in my life when I felt excluded or misjudged to imagine how they might feel.

I also believe it is beneficial to imagine how it feels to be the concerned father who is not sure he wants the topic of diversity introduced to his children. I imagine that he wants what is best for his children. He may feel some fear about introducing an alternative idea to his children because it might create pain and conflict for them.

In imagining the fears of the concerned parent, I join him in the feelings of wanting to protect and nurture our children. We can connect to each other's perspective through our concern for our children's well-being. When we recognize our common concern and feelings of protection, we can imagine children who encounter being teased or left out for an irrelevant reason—for example, how they look, feel, think, or talk. The child who has learned about diversity and bias will not internalize the negative experience as his or her fault. Instead, the child will have a perspective that allows him or her to see the negative experience as a symptom of the other person's ignorance.

As long as experiences such as these continue to occur, we have to be willing to confront bias and prejudice. We all have to work to create a culture of individuals who truly appreciate everything about who a person is, including being different from us.

Exercises:

- List the prejudices in you that you are aware of. Include both positive and negative ideas you have about specific groups of people.

CHAPTER FIVE

Applying Imagination to the Big Picture

I HAVE had the privilege of performing my play and introducing the imagination technique in a workshop for many divisions of a large banking corporation over the past two years. In every workshop, a variation on the same situation was always brought up. The situation involved a customer who would make prejudiced remarks about a teller and then refuse to work with him or her. In a playful way, using the tool of imagination on a large scale became the strongest intervention I could make. It took hearing several variations of the same question for me to discover how to use the imagination technique to push the envelope.

One of the bank's executive officers announced a policy that stated that if a customer refused to work with an employee because of a prejudice, the manager of that branch or office had the right to refuse to do business with the customer. The proactive antidiscrimination policy is one of the best examples I have found to indicate that positive changes are occurring with respect to bias in corporate America. Here is how the imagination tool helped employees accept that they could fire a customer because of the customer's refusal to refrain from prejudiced remarks and actions.

I was leading a discussion for a group of bank managers who worked in the rural areas of a Midwestern state. A bank manager raised his hand and described a typical scene: "I have a teller who is a black woman, and recently one of our customers refused to go to her when his turn came up. He said a lot of racist things while standing in line about working with her. I intervened and directed him to another teller who became available. What should I have done?"

The person who had hired me for that training, Laura, forcefully said: "You fire the customer because if you don't, you are undervaluing your employee. What message do you want to send to the people who work for you? Aren't they more important?"

At this point I was feeling a combination of anxiety and excitement because I knew we were dealing with a key issue. The room polarized immediately, with a lot of hands going up in defense of the bank manager. "Most of our customers are like that." "If we fired people like him we'd go out of business!"

For a while I became the referee between Laura and the vocal opponents of the new policy. As the room continued to heat up, I found my tool somewhere in my consciousness and asked everyone in the room to use the conflict as an opportunity to practice the tool. My personal bias would have made it easier to embellish how I imagined the African American employee might feel. After all, I was hired to help create a climate free of prejudice. I saw myself as a prejudice buster. I immediately wanted to side with Laura, who had spent several minutes talking about how the employee would have felt if the customer were simply redirected. I chose instead first to imagine how it felt to be the bank manager who felt obligated to cater to the customer's prejudices. I believed there would be more value in imagining how it felt to be the bank manager because I was in conflict with his response. I knew there would be more growth if I chose to imagine a perspective with which I was not comfortable.

I asked Laura to imagine, with other people's help, how the bank manger would feel about the possibility of losing a customer. We all began to paint quite vividly the fear of losing business and questioning the old axiom "the customer is always right." I watched as Laura and other employees (including me, on the "politically correct" side of the argument) began to feel

APPLYING IMAGINATION TO THE BIG PICTURE

real empathy toward the bank manager. I watched his defenses against the anticipated animosity soften. At that point I asked the bank manager and others to imagine how it felt to be Laura and the African American teller. The whole room got outside the conflict and saw the players and the questions in a human context. The conflict between the two sides was replaced by a connected group of people trying to solve a difficult problem.

At that point my imagination took another leap. As a way to assist the bank in defending the new policy, I said to everyone, "Imagine how your bank would be perceived if you did not honor the new policy." In my imagination, I flipped the policy around. I used the bank manager's fear and playfully took it to the other extreme. What if the bank policy stated that a manager was directed to satisfy a customer who continued to vocalize and act on his or her prejudice?

A commercial on the radio:

> Are you tired of being politically correct? Do you want people to realize that they can change your behavior but not your beliefs? Are you ready for a bank that will allow you not only to keep your prejudice but to act on it? Whatever happened to free-speech rights? Come to our bank, where we cater to your prejudices. You don't want a black banker, we'll give you a white one. You don't want a woman, we've got a man. You don't want one with a foreign accent, we have....

You get the picture. I pushed the envelope but it worked. It worked because the bankers in the audience had a chance to feel what it was like to be the black teller who was put aside in the name of the customer's prejudices. The role reversal was effective in getting people to understand the need for the bank's antidiscrimination policy, because we had already taken the time to connect with the bank manager's fear. The bank managers and employees were able to meet on the bridge of connection and accept the need for the bank's proactive stance against prejudice.

The imagination technique also needs to be applied to the African American coworker who was the target of a person's prejudices. Even if the manager has stepped in and dealt appropriately with the customer who vocalized his prejudices, it is vital to make a connection with the employee who was the target of the prejudiced remarks. Here is a scenario where the manager confronts the customer, Pat, appropriately:

> Pat: I'm gonna wait for a white teller. I want someone who is competent to handle my money.
>
> Manager: Excuse me, Pat. Everyone at my bank is professional and competent.
>
> Pat: Hey, if I don't want to give my money to a black teller, I don't have to.
>
> Manager: Pat, I need to ask you to step into my office.
>
> *(The scene changes to the office, where the customer and the manager can talk privately.)*
>
> Manager: I am trying to imagine how it feels to be someone who has banked here a long time and seen the community and the staff go from being almost exclusively people with the skin color of white to a wide variety of skin colors and accents.
>
> Pat: It sucks. I don't trust them.
>
> Manager: I believe you, and that is what I believe I saw today. Pat, everyone we have hired is competent, trustworthy, and professional. I have full confidence in my staff, and for you to continue to do your banking with us you need to refrain from stating your negative beliefs about my employees, and to follow the same rules as everyone else. The next teller available is the one you will work with.
>
> Pat: Hey, you can't tell me what to believe. I'll just let the person behind me work with them and I'll wait for a white teller.
>
> Manager: Not in this bank. If I allowed that behavior to occur, imagine what I would be saying about the value of the individuals who work for me. And yes, you are right, I cannot change your beliefs, but we will not cater to your prejudices either.

Pat: So what are you going to do?

Manager: If you are not willing to treat everyone here with respect, then I need to ask you to do your banking with another institution.

(Scene ends.)

The missing piece in this scenario is the African American teller who was the target of the customer's disrespect. It would be easy and quite human of the manager and other coworkers to end the conversation with "good riddance," but the employee would still be left with her feelings. If no one attempts to interact with her, she is left holding in her pain and bracing for the next time it may happen, not necessarily in the bank, but on her way home, perhaps.

Someone needs to try to connect with her. Ideally, a coworker or the manager would invite her into a private area for a break, and check in with "How're you doing?" After she responded, the imagination technique might come into play. "I would imagine that you might be feeling hurt, violated, distrustful...." Whatever words were used, the teller could either disagree and further clarify her own feelings ("No, not so much hurt as angry"), or feel supported ("That's it, that is how I feel right now"). Suddenly both people would be engaged in trying to communicate what the experience felt like. The teller would have the chance to express her feelings and move on. The coworker would have an opportunity to connect emotionally with how it would feel to have someone make a judgment based on something completely irrelevant to competence.

I wish more companies around the country committed themselves to a policy of not catering to a person's prejudices. The fear is that the companies would lose customers, but I believe an antidiscrimination policy applied to customers would create business. Almost everyone in this country has felt excluded at one time in his or her life. If a company actively stated that it was the policy not to cater to people's prejudices, I believe that people who have felt marginalized, disenfranchised, or just simply excluded would take their business to that company.

I also have seen how valued the employees in this banking corporation feel. People who work there will more likely be loyal, productive, and committed employees. Productivity and the bottom line have to increase because the time and money spent on hiring and recruiting is decreased. When an employee feels valued, there will be less turnover. Business not as usual—firing a customer who wants people to cater to his or her prejudices—is a smart way to do business.

Exercises:

- Imagine a customer has said a prejudiced remark to you. The manager tries to solve the problem by simply having the customer work with another teller. How do you feel?
- Does your company tolerate prejudice when it comes from a customer? What is the most proactive stance your workplace can take toward discrimination with respect to employment practices and customers? What are you willing to do to urge your company to take that stance?

CHAPTER SIX

Connecting with Emily

DURING the interview process for *Not until You Know My Story*, I started to wonder if I should interview a person with a disability. My wondering was followed with: "But I don't know anyone who has a disability." I realized that I had never known anyone with a disability. When I was a child I was sheltered not just from people of different races and ethnicities but from people with disabilities. I called several friends who I thought might know someone with a disability whom I could interview. None of my contacts had a current relationship with a person with a disability. It dawned on me that I would have to search to find someone I could include in my play about diversity. I also began to get in touch with my assumptions about a person with a disability. The assumptions I had formed went unchallenged because of my lack of interaction with people with disabilities. That there is a disproportionately high rate of unemployment among people with disabilities (four times the national average) creates an environment ripe for assumptions: the lack of direct contact.

One night I was attending a fund-raising event for the G.A.P. Theater Company in downtown Seattle. G.A.P. had worked with the American Red Cross on a play focusing on the effect of tobacco advertising on teenage smokers. As I was leaving the theater with my husband, I saw, out of the corner of my eye, a young woman with a Red Cross name tag in a wheelchair.

I felt uncomfortable noticing her, so I turned away. Then I thought, "Wait a minute, I am trying to create a play about people who are different from me. I should go talk to her." I looked at her again and noticed that her body was slightly twisted. I felt a vague sense of uneasiness bordering on nausea. I turned away again and thought, "This is incredible. I can't even look her in the eye." I was surprised and disturbed by the possibility of another emerging prejudice. I forced myself to walk up to her and introduce myself. I fumbled and mumbled "excuse me" a few times. Once I began to talk, I calmed down a bit. I managed to tell her who I was and what I was doing with my play. I started to realize that she was a person, which was a profound revelation at the time. I said, "I am interviewing people who are different from me for a play I am creating. I wondered if I could meet with you sometime to do an interview."

Emily smiled. She responded in a voice that sounded strained and distorted to me: "I'd love to. You can call me at the Red Cross. My name is Emily." I understood every word and somehow felt pleased with myself, as if that were an accomplishment. I smiled and said, a bit too warmly for our first contact, "GREAT! I'll call you soon."

I met with Emily the following week. I listened to her talk about what it was like to be her. I began to laugh and then to gasp as her experiences forced me to confront my assumptions about people with disabilities. One of the most memorable moments was when she described what she would do if someone who was trying to help her accidentally caused her to fall out of her wheelchair. I felt terror at what might happen if I were the person who caused her to fall. I thought, "Oh my God, she would be permanently injured. She might break. She would scream in agony and pain." Her answer was: "I'd just start laughing and then I'd get back in my chair and go on with the rest of my day. People are too worried, because really, we are all just human."

I was caught. One of my biggest assumptions was that people who had a disability were more fragile and needed me to feel sorry for them.

As I got to know Emily during subsequent interviews and later on as I portrayed her character on stage, the other big assumption that inhibited my ability to deal with a person who had a disability was to overadmire her for "carrying on so nobly." I would think, "She is just so amazing for having a sense of humor and living her life." If I truly imagined how it would feel to be her I might discover that if I were she I would not want to be overadmired for living my life.

I had already asked Emily to tell me her story and tried to imagine what it was like. Unfortunately, my imaginings were laced with assumptions. I assumed that she spent every day regretting that she had cerebral palsy. I imagined how hard it must be to accomplish simple tasks or to find humor in situations when you have a "hardship." My assumptions, although couched in trying to imagine how it felt to be her, really led me nowhere other than where I had been when I didn't know a person with a disability.

I decided that I should really try on her shoes. How would I feel if someone came up to me at an event with a look in his or her eyes that said, "I feel so sorry for you. How do you manage to face each day being who you are?" How would I feel if someone came up to me and asked with intense sympathy, "What happened to you?" I would feel outraged. I know who I am and accept who I am. How dare you feel sorry for me? I love my life. Suddenly I became aware of the concept of dignity as my assumptions were replaced with truly imagining how it felt.

The same was true with my excessive admiration of people with disabilities. If someone came up to me and said, "I am so impressed with how you managed to travel all the way here and do your job. I just admire you so much for that," I would feel outrage. I would feel infuriated. Please do not admire me for attributes you would expect from a professional employee. Admire me for my skill and expertise. I am an adult and fully capable of getting where I need to be to do my job. I may have different needs, but that is totally irrelevant to my ability to function as a responsible adult.

Imagining how it would feel to be with people who feel sorry for me or overadmire me makes it almost impossible for me to continue with those behaviors. My perspective has evolved to the shocking realization that a person with a disability probably wants to be treated simply as another human being. I can let go of perceiving a person with a disability as a "special" human being with a separate and mysterious set of rules because he or she must be "fragile" or "superhuman."

I repeatedly noticed that audience members would respond to the character of Emily in a different way than to all my other characters. Emily's jokes were not laughed at openly. I would see someone start to laugh and then try to hide the laughter with a hand or by looking down. She would try to make eye contact the way my other characters did, but people would look away or look at her with an expression of amazement or discomfort. I found the difference in reaction to her to be so severe that after a year of performing the play, I knew it was time to do a play that focused solely on people with both visible and invisible disabilities. I also realized I needed to create a play about disabilities so that I could confront my own assumptions through imagining how it felt to be the people about whom I made the assumptions.

I talked with an actor/playwright friend of mine, Anthony Curry, who had raised an autistic son. Tony had story after story of how he and his son had been misjudged, patronized, and ignored by people and the education system. He had a passion to confront the biases people with disabilities face, not just because of his son's experience but because of his own encounters with people who treated him differently when they found out about his son. The discrimination and misguided attempts to be helpful affect family members as well as the person with the disability. We decided to write and perform a play that would begin to address physical, emotional, and societal access issues for people with disabilities.

Tony and I met with people who were blind, who were in chairs, who had Lou Gehrig's disease, who were deaf, who were vocally impaired, who were developmentally delayed, who had hearing loss, and who had cerebral palsy. The issue of their disability quickly receded as they shared their lives so openly with us. I laughed and cried with people about their relationships and the experiences we all had in common. I would come home from an interview and tell my husband that I had just met a couple he would love. Suddenly I was developing relationships with people whom I never would have encountered if I had not set out to do a play about people with disabilities. I also met my assumptions over and over again. The good news about my assumptions was that I had learned a way not to let them dictate my responses and reactions. As long as I listened and imagined how it might feel, my need to turn away from or overadmire or feel sorry for others left me.

Marlaina and Gary are one of the couples with whom I have continued to stay in touch. Their love story was so enthralling that Tony and I decided to write a screenplay about their colorful and rich lives. Marlaina was a vocal advocate for disability and other civil rights who became immersed in the protest movement in the early 1970s. She had been blind since birth. She could be found with her guide dog in a human chain around a bus in San Francisco or on the floor of the Department of Health, Education, and Welfare in D.C. to address accessibility issues. Gary began as a conservative air force cargo pilot in Vietnam. Three months after retiring from the air force, he dove into a swimming pool and became quadriplegic. He met Marlaina on the Internet in a chat room about sexuality and disabilities. Several people in the movie industry told me that a story about two people with disabilities was not marketable to the general public. In trying to find an agent or producer for the screenplay, I had a taste of the rage I would feel if people always focused on my disability rather than my ability. Tony and I had found a great story, but because the people in the story happened to have disabilities, it would not sell.

Tony and I wrote the play *Not Just Ramps* based on the words and lives of the people we had met in the interviews. As actors we attempted to take on the physicality of each character as much as possible in an attempt to imagine how it felt to be them. When Marlaina heard the play, she wept and shared with us how she would never have thought it possible that two people without disabilities could effectively portray the issues she experienced every day. She agreed to join us to contribute her expertise and experience as a trainer in the workshop following the play.

In creating and performing *Not Just Ramps*, I discovered a whole group of people who are still being systematically disenfranchised. The level of disenfranchisement is reminiscent of how white people in power responded to skin-color differences in the late 1950s. A person in a wheelchair often has to enter a public place through the back door. There are still many activities that go on in buildings that are inaccessible for people in chairs unless they are willing to be carried. The people with disabilities in one school were moved to a portable classroom at the edge of campus where they would have little chance to interact with the rest of the student population. The unemployment rate for people with disabilities who are actively seeking work is three times that of people who are not disabled. Among blind people, the unemployment rate is between seventy-five and eighty percent.[2] An unemployment rate that high would be enough to cause a revolution in other countries. It would be impossible to marginalize people to this extreme in this day and age if we truly imagined how it would feel to be them.

The Americans with Disabilities Act access laws may have been a victory for making the built environment more accessible, but unfortunately it did not affect people's perceptions and assumptions about people with disabilities. An employer may be required to build a ramp and widen a restroom stall, but there has still been little progress in educating an employer to realize that the benefits often far outweigh the costs of employing people with disabilities. Tony's son Adam was hired by a movie theater in the Seattle area. He was given a raise and more hours because movie patrons and coworkers could not help but feel the joy he brought to his work. He was good for their business.

---

[2] Statistics from the National Center for Dissemination of Disability Research.

The only way to affect our perceptions is through imagination and connection. I can imagine the urgency, passion, and anger I may encounter in a person who has to fight for the right to work, or to enter a building through the front door.

> *Exercises:*
>
> - Imagine you wake up one morning with a disability you do not already have. You are still able to work with the help of adaptive technology. Imagine how people treat you when you come to work. What do you want them to know about you?

CHAPTER SEVEN

Hitting Too Close to Home

I PERFORM a one-woman play in which I portray people who are different from me in obvious ways: skin color, religion, ethnicity, disability, language, size, sexual orientation, and privilege. I also portray my mother, who is not different from me in any of those ways, but she feels more different to me than all of the previous differences combined. She is different from me in perspective and belief, two invisible differences that I believe give many people the most difficulty when it comes to being willing to cross the bridge and make a real connection with another person. If the challenge and benefit of diversity lie in the moments when we are most uncomfortable with other people, then it is time that I imagine how it feels to be my mother.

Here are some moments in our relationship that capture our differences:

- My biggest shame as a white person: my ancestors owned slaves. My mother's biggest source of pride as a white person: my ancestors treated their slaves kindly.

- I continually question the concept that I was raised with that I could be superior to someone else because of my lineage. Recently my younger daughter and I stayed at my mother's house. I went into my mother's room, where Elsa was playing and talking with her. My mother asked: "Carrie, how would you define 'peasant' for Elsa?" When I explained that it was a word that has a connotation of inferiority and one I preferred not to use, my mother rolled her eyes and came back with: "Oh come on, there is nothing wrong with calling a person a peasant, is there?"

- The summer before the Gore-Bush presidential election, one of my sisters and I were having lunch with my mother. The subject turned to politics, which seems to be somewhat safe ground because my mother and I tend to agree on most political issues. She said, "Gore's speech was well received by the NAACP. That's good because everyone loves dogs." I spat out the water I was drinking and asked, "Mom? What do you think 'NAACP' stands for?" while hoping that no one would recognize me as a diversity trainer. She replied "Oh, isn't that the group who saves dogs?" I said "No, that would be the ASPCA." Fortunately, we were all raised with a sense of humor, and I continued with: "If I didn't realize that you had your acronyms confused, I might have interpreted that as the most racist comment I have ever heard." She laughed and said, "Oh my, that was a bit of a faux pas, wasn't it?"

I interviewed my mother for the play, and as an actor, I was pretty convinced I was doing a good job of becoming her. After all, I had been imitating her, as a good daughter does, most of my life, so I knew I was being accurate. My director, John Vreeke, respectfully disagreed. "You're making fun of her. I don't believe you."

I had no idea what he was talking about. I felt I was totally becoming my mother on stage. The truth was that my imitation of her was great, but I had not begun to walk across the bridge of imagination to connect with her feelings. I had spent most of my adult life making sure the ways we were not alike outweighed what we had in common. I wanted to be my own unique person, not "just like my mother." The last thing I wanted was to become her, or even imagine what it was like to be her; there's the rub. She was the only character whom, because of my own issues and biases, I had not let myself fully become.

I thought I was imagining what it was like to be my mother when I told John, "Oh, I know how she feels. She feels she is better than other people." My assumption is a perfect example of how people can think they are imagining how it feels but in reality are simply placing their attitudes and prejudices on other people. As I stated earlier, few people wake up in the morning and say to themselves, "Hmm, today I think I'll feel superior to everyone I meet." The obvious clue that I was not really imagining how it felt to be my mother was that I answered his question immediately, without any thought.

Imagining how it feels to be somebody else, especially someone whom you do not want to be, is difficult. It takes thought, vulnerability, and effort to put yourself in someone else's shoes. The struggle and at times emotional pain of trying to imagine that person's feelings create a human connection. I had a breakthrough with the character of my mother when I really put myself in her shoes and responded in a more thoughtful way. I said, "She might feel some pride and contentment knowing her lineage. Her family line is an important part of her identity. She may feel some hurt and confusion in response to my attempts to detach myself from our family's inherited privilege." As I struggled to imagine my mother's feelings, I suddenly felt as though I were really looking through her eyes, as opposed to bringing all my prejudices about her into my portrayal of her.

My attempts to imagine how it felt to be my mother helped me see how much more we had in common than I was willing to accept before I used the technique of imagining. The good news is that now I know myself better and can have a healthier relationship with her. I still forget, at times, to cross the bridge. I also find myself wishing she would cross the bridge and imagine life from my shoes. In the moments when I wish she could try to see life from my perspective I feel more cold or distant toward her. The sense of isolation that comes from feeling the distance between us is not particularly healthy for my own sense of well-being. The act of imagining how it feels to be my mother, crossing the imagination bridge and standing in her shoes, creates a warmer connection with her and is good medicine for me.

> *Exercises:*
>
> - Pick a person in your life who is different from you in perspective and belief. Using your imagination, write a letter to yourself from him or her about your differences.

CHAPTER EIGHT

Our Attachment to Irritation

WHY IS it that we humans find it easier to be irritated at someone else than to try to make a connection with the person who is irritating us? The preference for irritation rather than connection is a mystery to me. Unfortunately, I still opt for irritation in many interactions I have with people on a daily basis.

When I am performing *Not until You Know My Story* for corporations around the country, I frequently travel and will often crawl into my "I want to be productive so get out of my way" mode when I am on a plane or train. Recently when traveling by train I heard a mother talking to her three-month-old baby in a loud, syrupy voice. "Oh honey, I know you hate to visit your aunt, but we have to. Your aunt has great big control issues, doesn't she?" Or, "Look, baby, that's where Mommy used to have that awful job where they never paid her enough." I started to squirm, thinking, "Who does she think that child is, her therapist?" I felt my mild irritation grow into self-righteous disgust. The more I pointedly ignored the mother and her loud confessions, the more I noticed an increase in my intolerance level. I even thought that if I ignored the mother really well, she might get the message that her child and the rest of the people on the train did not want to hear about her "issues."

Suddenly I remembered that I was on my way to a training where I would be talking about the power of imagining how it felt to be other people who, because of difference, may be a source of irritation or discomfort to us. I began to entertain the possibility that I might not have to spend the rest of my journey in the "divine state of irritation." I needed to look at the mother and try to feel the love she had for her child, and perhaps her loneliness. Maybe she kept sharing intimate details about her life and her relationships with her three-month-old baby because she did not have other adults in her life in whom to confide. The mother wanted to share her thoughts as a way to make a connection with another person. I realized that my irritation was subsiding as I recognized the feeling of wanting to connect with a friend or my partner. It did not mean that I now had to be one of the adults with whom the mother could have an intimate conversation. I could still have my time alone, but without the high dose of irritation.

A great example of people's reluctance to transform their irritation into connection came from one of my earliest trainings. After the play I asked people in the audience to pick someone in their lives who irritated them. I then had the audience members imagine how it felt to be the person who was a source of their negative feelings. When the exercise was over, I asked if anyone had a discovery he or she would like to share with the other participants. In the back of the room a woman's hand shot straight up in the air. She practically leapt out of her seat. She said, "Oh my God. I have just had an epiphany!" I was excited since this would be my first participant "epiphany." She continued:

> I work in a cubicle that is located near the copy machine. Every day this woman comes down to make copies. After a few minutes she starts to talk to the machine. Then she talks louder and cusses at the machine. She hits it a few times and then walks away when there has been a paper jam or when the machine is out of paper. I sit there fuming because she is so loud and disruptive. I can't get any of my work done. This has been going on for months.

> Then I imagined how it felt to be her. I just discovered that maybe she doesn't know how the copy machine works. And you know what? Next time she comes to the copy machine, I'm going to help her!

The woman collapsed back in her chair in the afterglow of her discovery.

Although the participant's discovery seems obvious, many of us in a similar situation would continue to feel irritated and disrupted rather than try to interact and emotionally connect with the woman who had daily fights with the copy machine. For me, it might not be the person at a copy machine, but it could easily be the airline ticket agent for a plane that had been delayed. If only I could remember to imagine how it felt to be the ticket agent who is always the target of customers' frustrations with the airline, before I wallowed in my irritation, then we both would end up experiencing a more positive interaction.

Exercises:

- Pick a mildly irritating experience you had recently, a time where a stranger did or said something that bothered you. What do you imagine was going on in that stranger's mind and heart at that moment?

CHAPTER NINE

Bridging a Polarity

ONE OF the biggest polarities that I have come across in corporate America and in schools is the gap between people who advocate for gay and lesbian rights and people who come from a religious perspective that believes homosexuality is a sin.

The gap between the two positions is so wide that until two years ago I had witnessed and participated in hundreds of unsuccessful interactions between people on both sides of the conflict. In my seven years of touring my plays to schools with the G.A.P. Theater Company, the issue polarized the room almost every time.

G.A.P. actors routinely shared their own experiences with discrimination after each performance as a way to open up the discussion. One of the actors, Rob, used his experience of being a gay man as a door to walk through to imagine how it felt to be a person of color in this country. After the first few postplay discussions, parents with strong religious views about homosexuality began to voice their disapproval with his disclosure. We were then asked by several schools to do our play without allowing Rob to share his identity.

The first day a school made the request to leave Rob's disclosure out of the discussion, every member of the company had to struggle with a difficult question. Could we perform a play about discrimination and at the same time treat one actor differently by asking him not to share who he was? After many painful discussions, we unanimously agreed that we would not perform the play if people asked us to censor our discussion. Our decision led to an ongoing battle with people who felt that homosexuality was a sin. The G.A.P. Theater Company began to receive phone calls to cancel bookings. I was told of a school board meeting at which five hundred parents from other school districts showed up to protest a theater company that "promoted homosexuality." I was shown a questionnaire from Washington State's Christian Coalition asking its members whether it was a wise use of its funds to focus on a campaign that would force the G.A.P. Theater Company to go out of business.

I responded to their effort to try to destroy the company with a righteous adamancy that there was no way to communicate with a person who held the view that homosexuality was a sin. When I facilitated a discussion and a person in the audience talked from the perspective of homosexuality being a sin, I would thank the person for sharing and move on, or plead with him or her to try to feel the pain that viewpoint was creating in other people. As the battles continued, I simply turned up the volume and tried to change those beliefs by becoming more passionate about gay and lesbian rights. After leaving the G.A.P. Theater Company, I finally admitted how ineffective my "interventions" had been.

During the discussion following *Not until You Know My Story*, the polarity between people who believed homosexuality was a sin and people who were advocates for gay and lesbian rights presented itself again. This time I was ready to try something new. I was scheduled to do the play and training for a group of human resource professionals who represented specific sites in their company throughout North America. I was told that the people in the room had not only participated in diversity trainings but were in charge of conducting diversity trainings for their specific regions. Right before my presentation, the person who had hired me took me aside and said, "I think we are going to need more time before you begin. There is a conflict that has just come up and we need to talk about it." Ready to experiment with my tool of imagination, I daringly said, "Please, don't deal with it. Let me do the play and then I will use the discussion to work through the conflict." She looked skeptical but agreed, and the show went on.

After the play I set the parameters for the discussion and talked about the tool of imagining how it felt to be someone else. Then I went straight for the conflict. The following is an excerpt from the discussion:

Carrie: Okay, I was told before I started that there was a conflict in the room. Who would like to fill me in?

(Silence.)

Carrie: Aha. Okay. What was it about?

(Silence. Please note that the people in the room were trainers themselves, adept at conflict resolution.)

Carrie: All right, I do have some idea what it is about. There is someone in this room who has strong religious views about homosexuality and there is someone in the room who feels offended by that. Will you let me know who you are?

(Silence, with a few uncomfortable giggles.)

Carrie: Great.

(I am now feeling a bit anxious about the productivity of the discussion thus far.)

Carrie: Okay, let's try something. I want everyone to put yourself in the shoes of the person who stated their belief that homosexuality is a sin.

(Silence. I watched as many of the people in the room squirmed. Their faces showed traces of shock and surprise that a trainer who was here to deal with discrimination asked them to empathize with a person who had made a discriminatory remark.)

Carrie: How do you think it feels to be that person who shared their religious beliefs with this group?

(Finally, someone spoke.)

Sam: Maybe they feel anxious about what we're going to think.

Sandra: Possibly fear of being isolated.

Anne: Fear of being ostracized, or persecuted.

(Then it happened; the person we were talking about felt safe enough to identify himself.)

Rich: Okay, it was me. And yeah, I am feeling some of those things. It was a big risk for me to share my discomfort. I'm not supposed to feel uncomfortable about homosexuality. I'm in human resources.

Carrie: Thanks for coming into the discussion. Will you try something with me now, with everyone else's help, of course?

Rich: I guess.

(I was aware that for the first time I was not dismissing his viewpoint. I definitely disagreed with it, but that was not relevant here.)

Carrie: Let's try to imagine how it feels to be the person who felt offended by your comments.

Rich: Maybe he feels some of the same kind of fear, fear of being persecuted, fear of isolation.

(Another man raised his hand.)

Don: Rich, that's right. That is how I feel. I never realized that you had similar feelings

Rich and Don shared the feelings that lay underneath the conflict over homosexuality because we had all become engaged in trying to imagine how it felt to be them. As people in the room connected with both sides of the conflict, a bridge was built. Neither Rich nor Don wanted to continue the discussion at that point because they wanted to experience what they had in common: their feelings.

The technique of imagining worked. If Rich and Don worked together on the same team, the discovery that they had similar feelings underneath their conflicting beliefs would help them find a place of connection. The experience of feeling connected allowed both of them to feel safe about bringing their whole selves to work. When people bring their whole selves to work, they are more productive because they have more energy and commitment.

> *Exercises:*
>
> - Pick an issue where you have been in passionate disagreement with another person. What do you imagine the person, who has a point of view you adamantly disagree with, is thinking and feeling?

CHAPTER TEN

The "I Love My Opinions" Obstacle

AFTER a year of touring my play, I realized that I had had only a handful of reactions in which people would express anger and defensiveness toward me and the characters I portrayed. Almost all of the people who felt angry told me that they felt as if my play had purposely left their viewpoints out. These people told me they were religious and had strong views about homosexuals that they were not allowed to express openly in the workplace. I decided to challenge myself to use the technique of imagining by finding a person to interview and portray who had beliefs that were completely opposite to my own. In the summer of 1999, the perfect candidate emerged during a postplay discussion at a community performance. I called on a man who was sitting in the back of a large room filled with students from all the high schools in the valley where I live. Pastor Steven Maxwell spoke passionately to the audience and me about how offended he was that the Jewish character in my play implied that Southern Baptists were against Jewish people. The Jewish man in my play states:

> The Southern Baptists, the second largest religion in this country, said their number one priority was to convert Jews to Jesus. If an organized religion is actually vocalizing that and the nonevangelical Christians are keeping silent, are afraid, or don't understand why it's important to say, "No, that's not right, we don't want a world like that," then I

can't see why we won't have violence in the future against anyone who doesn't accept Jesus!

After the discussion I cautiously approached Steven and asked if I could interview him and incorporate his character in the play. Steven enthusiastically gave me his card and we agreed to meet the following week. As I walked away, I looked down at his card: Steven S. Maxwell, pastor of the local Baptist church. I felt as if I needed to prepare for a big final exam.

On the morning of the interview, I kept reminding myself that I had to interview him without judgment. I would say to myself, "Carrie, you have to leave all your opinions at the door." The other side of me would argue back, "But I love my opinions. I have spent years creating them and I am quite fond of them." I responded with, "Look, I am not saying you have to agree with him. Your opinions will be waiting for you as soon as the interview is finished."

I made myself promise to suspend my opinions, and with that assurance I drove down to the church. I found Steven sitting in a pew with three other people, singing the tenor part of a hymn. His voice was rich and beautiful. He was a singer who loved to make music. I allowed myself to breathe a little more deeply and think, "We have something in common because I also love to sing." As we walked to his office he told me about how his family grew up singing. I shared my love of harmonizing with people. The singing conversation got us pleasantly to our seats.

I turned on the tape recorder and asked Steven to tell me about his life, his faith, his passions, and his beliefs. For an hour I listened intently without judgment. I successfully repressed all my judgments about his views on the sin of homosexuality and the need for Jewish people to embrace the Christian church. My judgments were waiting for me outside the door of his office. Steven seemed to enjoy my questions. As the interview came to a conclusion, he went over to his bookshelf and reached for a Bible. He said, "Carrie, I want you to do something. I want you to read the following passages . . . and then, if you would like to come on back, we can talk some more."

THE "I LOVE MY OPINIONS" OBSTACLE

    I took the Bible and thanked him. I felt pleased with myself because his comment meant that I had been somewhat successful in listening to him without judgment.

    I was surprised how easy the interview was—until I got to my car. As I drove away I began to rehear the conversation. My body began to shake involuntarily. At first I had no idea what I was feeling. Then I realized that the physical sensation in my body was fear. I felt terrified. The feeling lasted for three hours or so. Up until that interview, I had no idea that what I was asking people to do, the act of imagining how it feels to be someone else, could be terrifying. Why does the technique of imagining how it feels to be other people create fear? Leaving our opinions out of a conversation is potentially difficult because we fear we will lose our identities. I was frightened when I got back to my car because I felt as if the result of suspending my judgment was that I had become him. The truth is I did no such thing. I did not become him, nor did I agree with him; I simply took a vacation from my opinions in order to communicate. The act of imagining how it felt to be Steven while he talked let me focus on him, not my own judgments and opinions. I was able to listen to him fully without the filtering effect of my biases.

    Although I was able to sustain the state of listening to his words without judgment for short periods of time, his words were the most difficult for me to memorize. My attention kept wandering; I was unable to focus. I even called my director several times to tell him that I had decided that there was no need to add Steven to the play. I finally absorbed Steven's words by forcing myself to try to imagine his feelings and thoughts behind the words. I always need to imagine a character's thoughts and feelings in order to memorize lines, but I was still trying to resist imagining Steven's internal process because I disagreed with his words so intensely. As Steven calmly and confidently talked about homosexuality, I kept finding myself thinking about the potential pain and destruction his words could cause in the life of a young person struggling with his or her orientation. Steven states:

God has set some standards and you cannot escape that fact, especially as pertains to homosexuality, in particular, because God calls that clearly, in the Old Testament and in the New Testament, an unnatural perversion, because it's against nature, against the creative order. The Book of Revelation talks about the fact that homosexuals cannot inherit the kingdom of God.

I have been portraying Steven for months, and people often focus on his character as a source of anger. I recently did the play and training for a group of government employees in Washington. I had just finished explaining how I chose to do the play so I could model the technique of imagining how it feels to be other people, when a woman's hand went up. She said, "I think the character of Steven is false. He seems so secure, like he really enjoys being who he is. Where is his pain? He doesn't feel pain!"

This woman had a hard time imagining that someone with such a different viewpoint could conceivably like who he was, because she obviously did not like what he represented. She wanted him to feel pain, possibly because she experienced pain in her life. She wanted him to be insecure.

Another woman, Deborah, who had some relatives who were killed in the Holocaust, followed this woman's comment. Tears came to Deborah's eyes as she stated that the character of Steven and his beliefs caused her pain. The room was totally silent. I sat in the silence, imagining some of the horror his comments about wanting Jewish people to accept Jesus as the savior caused her. He states:

> You may not know this, but we have such a love for the Jewish people, and that the Jews are against us is so ironic. Jesus was a Jewish man. And we believe he is their messiah. Every writer of the New Testament is Jewish except for Luke. It is a thoroughly Jewish book.
>
> As Christians we have access to the Gospel because Jews rejected Christ. God has always intended that the Jews be witness to the world for Christ. But no, they wanted to hold it to themselves. And so the Gentile church became the

greatest church as far as evangelism to the world. In Romans, Paul the apostle says, "Brothers, my heart's desire and my prayers for Israel is that they come to the knowledge of the truth of the gospel and be saved."

For Deborah, Steven's comments potentially meant the murder of her relatives and friends. I told her that I was imagining the pain, anger, and horror his words might be eliciting in her. She took a deep breath and acknowledged that my words had let her know I had heard her. Then I said to her and the other participants, "In moments like this, maybe it is okay to not make a connection, to not try to imagine how it feels to be someone other than you." Steven was in no way connected to the past history Deborah associated with his comments. Had Deborah imagined how it felt to be Steven, she may have realized this, but I felt that connecting to her pain was more important in order for her to be open to further dialogue.

If Deborah had to work with Steven, she would have to separate who he was from what had happened to her relatives. She would have to try to imagine some common feelings underneath his words. However, at that moment I knew the technique of imagining was meant only as a tool for me to use to connect with Deborah and acknowledge her pain.

My experience with Deborah took me back to another class with Julius Lester. We were not discussing people with different religious beliefs, but rather a much more extreme difference. A student asked Julius whether there was any value in imagining how it felt to be Hitler or other people who were responsible for extreme acts of violence. He advocated the power of imagining how it felt to be other people, but he also adamantly stated that there were moments when the act of trying to understand someone who was capable of evil was dangerous and could imply approval of the thought process that led to the destructive behavior.

So the only caution with the technique of imagining is this: *It is useful to try to imagine the context and the forces that may have created a person who is capable of evil, but to try to empathize with him or* her—to try to imagine how it feels to be that person—is dangerous because it borders on condoning the behavior and following the same path.

> *Exercises:*
>
> - Let yourself off the hook and acknowledge the people you may not want or need to make a connection with. You do not need to imagine how it feels to be them.

CHAPTER ELEVEN

I'll Save You, Nell

AFTER the first preview of *Not until You Know My Story* in 1997, a woman came up to me and made a compelling argument for including a woman in the play who spoke about gender issues. I tried to rationalize to her that I was a woman and the issue of gender was covered because I spoke about my own experience throughout the play. My rationalization succeeded in increasing her anger and adamancy that I was in denial about gender discrimination and that I needed to include a woman in the play who directly addressed the issue of gender bias. She walked away thoroughly dissatisfied because of my inability to empathize with her point of view. I left the conversation disturbed that I had defended the current form of my play and that I had resisted the inclusion of a new character mostly because I was anxious about the time and energy that a possible change implied.

A week later, I decided that gender discrimination needed to be addressed directly and that my resistance was a symptom of burnout, not reason. I immediately began to look for a woman whom I could interview. The first place I looked was a construction site where I noticed a crew of five men and one woman. I thought, "I bet she has some things to say." My image was that I would find a strong woman who confronted discrimination on a daily basis. I got out of my car and approached the torn-up pavement where she was working. I had to yell over the jackhammer that a man was using fifteen feet from where the female construction worker was standing.

> Carrie: Excuse me. I am writing a play about people who experience discrimination because of their differences. May I interview you?
>
> *(She yelled back.)*
>
> Woman: What do you want to talk about?
>
> Carrie: Do you get discriminated against because you are a woman?
>
> Woman: Yeah, I just tell them to fuck off. Anything else?
>
> *(She was obviously finished.)*
>
> Carrie: No, that will do it. Thanks.
>
> Woman: No problem.

I left discouraged that I would be able to find my ideal woman. Several days later, a friend of mine who worked at a major software company told me he had the perfect woman for me to interview. In fact, she was dying to talk about her experiences. I set up a telephone interview because she lived in California.

Nell described herself as a platinum-blonde-haired woman who loved to wear short dresses and costume jewelry. She spoke in a high voice that bordered on a whine. She was not my idea of the strong woman whom I wanted to speak for my gender. After spending an hour on the phone with her, I realized she was the character I had been looking for. The play was not about people representing people like them; the play was about individuals who simply told their stories. Although Nell appeared to be a stereotype, she was a real person who experienced an enormous amount of discrimination and disrespect on a daily basis. She was a biology major who was highly skilled technically in a work team made up entirely of men. She was ignored, she was made fun of, and frequently she was part of a group addressed as "gentlemen."

Nell became one of my most effective characters because audience members would express their impatience with and anger at her for not confronting the prejudice and disrespect that she experienced at work. Nell described numerous situations like the following one, in which she did not confront her coworkers.

> What I should have said to him was: "Well, gee, Tim, we're having a marketing meeting and it really does require a high level of people skills, so we are not going to invite you because you obviously don't have any." And I'd actually like to be that bold; to just put him flat on his butt. It is so outrageous to even remotely imply in front of everybody that I can't hold my own. I'd like to tell him to go to hell, but I don't do it. Instead I went home and cried.

Almost every time I do a training, people tell me that she should simply confront the behaviors. She should be strong; otherwise there is no reason for people to change. My response to people's frustration with her not being strong enough is to ask them what the value is in telling Nell to be stronger. They usually realize that she would probably just shut down.

If instead, as a coworker or supervisor of Nell, you try to imagine what might have happened to her to prevent her from defending herself, then a connection is made. I share with people that Nell has experienced blatant and subtle forms of bias at least five times a day for as long as she has worked for the software company. Imagine how hard it is to defend yourself when no one will look you in the eye or take you seriously.

The act of imagining her reality does two powerful things. It allows us to learn about the work culture and gender in a way that will involve both our intellect and our emotions. When we are engaged intellectually and emotionally, then we can become part of the solution. It also creates a connection with Nell, and through that connection she can join in the solution, perhaps because she feels supported for the first time.

Recently, Bill, a lawyer for a banking corporation, entered into a debate with me about the value of the technique of imagining as it related to Nell. He raised his hand after I began facilitating the discussion and with a broad smile said, "Carrie, I have to say that I don't really buy this empathy thing. Doesn't it just boil down to courtesy and character? Take Nell, for instance. If what she is saying is true, then I don't need to waste time empathizing with her, I should just take care of the problem. What's happening to her is wrong, so I should just fix it."

I spent time clarifying with Bill what courtesy and character meant to him. He spoke about respecting the dignity of every human being and making an honest connection with people. I realized that Bill was able to imagine how it felt to be Nell, but his immediate reaction to "getting it" was to fix the problem. He forced me to articulate why fixing the problem, or "saving Nell," without making an attempt to connect with her by trying to imagine how she felt, was not the most effective way to make a change in the corporate culture.

Bill's desire to save Nell would have two potentially negative outcomes. The first would be that, although he might succeed in stopping most of the discriminatory behavior she was experiencing, she would still not feel like part of the team. He would save her and do it in a way that would leave her out of the solution. She would continue to feel isolated and disconnected from her coworkers because no effort would have been made to forge a true connection with her. In her own eyes and the eyes of her coworkers, she would not be part of the solution, but simply the focus of the problem.

The other negative outcome would be in the feelings and attitudes of her coworkers. Their discriminatory behaviors might change for the most part, but because they had not been invited to imagine how it felt to be her, their attitudes would probably remain the same. They would not look for ways to include her; instead, they would simply "be good" and cooperate with the new rules of behavior set down by Bill.

I, like Bill, love to be a problem solver. However, if I rush to solve the problem before trying to make a connection with Nell, the culture remains unchanged. I feel strong and comfortable when I solve problems partly because I am in control. If Bill tried to connect with Nell by trying to imagine out loud how it felt to be her, he would be in unfamiliar territory. The solution that might evolve would not be his solution, but a solution born out of their connection and understanding. A mutually arrived-at solution would allow Nell to experience inclusion, perhaps for the first time, in the workplace.

> *Exercises:*
>
> - Think of a time when you tried to solve someone else's problem without making a connection in order to collaboratively solve it with them. Was it effective? How do you imagine the other person felt about your solution?

CHAPTER TWELVE

To Be PC or Not to Be PC

IMAGINING how it feels to be someone other than you is a communication tool that takes the place of the need to know all the "politically correct" words to use when speaking with someone who is different. In most of the workshops following the play, a person will say: "How can I talk anymore without offending someone? There is so much emphasis on using the right term that I am scared to say anything."

This chapter applies the tool of imagining how it feels to be another person to language. Creating a connection is not about being right or wrong. Connection is about the process of imagining and the dialogue that we engage in during the process. Language is a wonderful opportunity to look at the concept of inclusion, not an anxiety-filled challenge to be avoided.

I, however, did avoid the opportunity when I was teaching drama to teenagers at a summer program at the University of Washington. The program was designed to prepare low-income high school students for entrance to the university. I was hired as the drama teacher. The students in my class chose to develop a play about their experience of racism. The class was divided evenly between black and white students. Three students chose to do a scene from a Spike Lee script in which "nigga" was used several times. The young people I was working with referred to each other as "nigga" and adamantly defended the difference between "nigga" as a term of affection and "nigger," the racist slur. As the rehearsal process proceeded, the students got in touch with their own feelings of anger about the racism they had experienced. The students' feelings and experiences began to spill into other classrooms and eventually into the weekly teacher meeting.

The teacher meeting began with the usual business and then quickly focused on the drama class. The focus was unusual, because the meeting time was normally reserved for the "academic" subjects. I began to defend the intense emotion of the students in response to the teachers' concerns that the emotions were counterproductive to their academic learning. The temperature in the room drastically changed when one teacher, Barbara, specifically asked me about the use of "nigga." She told me that, as an African American woman, she was very offended that I would allow the students to use that word at all.

I immediately became self-righteously defensive. I was twenty-seven and had not yet realized the power of the technique of imagining to open a constructive dialogue. I told her that it was part of the script, that the students chose the scene, and that I would not engage in censorship. Barbara told me again, with more intensity, that she was offended and did not want the word used at all. I responded with more adamancy about the need to honor the students' choices. I explained the students' distinction between "nigga" and "nigger." I left that day feeling angry that she did not understand the students' point of view or the need to present the scene as it was written. The truth, in hindsight, is that I was the one who did not understand the complexity of using the word, whether "nigg" ended in "a" or "er."

Eight years later, my experience in the teacher meeting came back to me in a new light thanks to an actor in the G.A.P. Theater Company. Edmonia was a sixty-two-year-old African American woman who had a way of asking questions that demanded soul-searching honesty. Edmonia was a retired school principal and had started her second career as an actor and jazz singer. One day she allowed five hundred high school students and six other actors in our company to get a glimpse of the pain she felt while growing up in the 1940s in the South.

We had performed *The Hurt of One*, a play about racism in high school. In the postplay discussion, a white student asked, "How come it's okay for a black person to say 'nigga,' but if we say it it's not?" Various students got into the discussion. One African American student explained the distinction between "a" and "er." He said he had every right to use the word ending in "a" and that it was unrelated to the derogatory term. The argument continued until Edmonia decided to go to a place that none of us had seen before, the place where she was still a hurt young girl. Her voice quivered with emotion as she described how at the age of twelve she had witnessed a man being tarred and feathered. Between choked pauses, she described the smell of burning flesh and the sound of anguished cries for help as the backdrop for hearing the men responsible use the N-word over and over again. As the tears began to fall down her cheeks onto the stage, she said: "That is what happens to me when I hear the word. I go back there. I relive every moment. I don't care who uses it. I don't care if it ends in an 'a' or an 'er.' It hurts."

The room went silent as Edmonia showed us her pain. The argument stopped and many of the students and all of the actors had a moment to imagine the pain the N-word created for some people.

Edmonia cried and moaned for two hours after that presentation with my husband and me as we drove home. She needed to release the pain and horror she had experienced as she watched the tarring and feathering of another human being. The twelve-year-old girl in her had never put words to her pain until that day in the high school. She was willing to touch that pain to get the high school students to listen to her. As she cried I realized that no matter what my good intentions were, censorship or student rights, I would never again be a part of defending anyone's right to use that word. Edmonia's willingness to touch her pain acted like a hammer to pierce my defensiveness and try to imagine what Barbara, the African American teacher, might have felt in confronting me eight years earlier. If I had simply asked her how the word affected her and then tried to imagine how she felt, there might have been a different outcome. A different outcome would have forced an important and difficult conversation with the students I was teaching. Unfortunately, the opportunity for that conversation was missed because I stubbornly stayed on what I thought was the "right" side.

Recently, both experiences came to mind during a postplay discussion of *Not until You Know My Story*. Ella described an experience she had recently gone through; a customer came into her office and was shocked to find out that she was not white. The customer told Ella that she "had sounded Caucasian on the telephone." Ella expressed her hurt and anger to the group.

A man with a Polish accent, Frank, responded to Ella with a hypothetical example. He wanted to make Ella feel better. He said that if a person said he "sounded like a nigger" on the telephone, then he would ask the person what that sounded like. Several people in the room, including me, flinched at his use of the N-word. I wanted to intervene and point out that his story was giving Ella a solution before connecting with her through the act of imagining. I started to ask the participants to imagine how it felt to be Ella, when another African American woman raised her hand. She took a deep breath and attempted to swallow the obvious emotion she was feeling. She confronted Frank on his use of the N-word. She said she was offended by it. Frank responded in the same way I had in the teacher meeting. He said, "I wasn't using it in a prejudiced way, I was just making a point." The woman repeated that it had offended her. I stopped Frank from further defending his use of the word and invited him and everyone else to try to imagine what might be going on for the woman who had confronted him. As people began to fill in what they thought she might be feeling, she shared her deep hurt and allowed herself to show some of the emotions she had tried to swallow earlier. Frank became very quiet; his need to defend his position was gone.

At the end of the session, Frank stood up and said: "I need to say something. I apologize for using the word I used, and I want everyone here to know that I will never use it again."

Several people in the room responded with tears and spontaneous applause. Frank got it. As soon as he let go of the need to defend himself, and instead focused on what the African American woman might be feeling, there was space for not only a good dialogue, but also behavioral change.

Frank did not go into the training worried about saying the wrong thing. He simply said what he was thinking. Frank used an example that he thought was powerful and would prove a positive response to Ella's situation. Fortunately, a person in the room was willing to take a risk and say that Frank's example had offended her. The moment when his language was considered to be offensive led to a wonderful opportunity. When Frank was invited to imagine how it felt to be the woman who had confronted him, everyone in the room gained new insight about the power of a word. Frank put himself in the woman's shoes. Now he has an emotional memory attached to the N-word that came from the act of imagining. The feelings he imagined will most likely lead to a different word choice in the future and a greater sensitivity to language. Frank's emotional memory is much more likely to prevent him from using offensive language than memorizing the *correct* vocabulary word would have.

My response to people's anxiety over language is twofold. First, do not use words that you know are offensive. Second, do not let your fear of saying the wrong thing stop you from talking with people who are different. Ideally, I can enter a conversation knowing that I may unintentionally say something that offends the other person. Once I have noticed that the person looks distant or offended, I use that as an opportunity.

"I noticed you looked distant just now. Did I say something that offended you?" The person can say, "Well, yes, you did. You said...." Here is the opportunity I have been waiting for. Instead of saying, "Oh, you misunderstood me," I can respond with "Can I try to imagine how you felt when you heard me say that?" The conversation that will follow will be fresh and full of growth for both of us. Instead of defending myself, I will gain a deeper understanding of the effect of language. The other person will have the pleasure of talking with someone who is open to change rather than armed with defenses to stay the same. Moments at which my ignorance may lead to offense can be reframed in my mind into opportunities to cross the bridge of connection.

> *Exercises:*
>
> - Remember a moment when someone confronted you with saying something they felt offended or hurt by. Write your response to them starting with "I imagine you may have felt _____ when you heard me say that." Make sure your response does not contain any hidden defensiveness.

CHAPTER THIRTEEN

The "If Only" Moments

I AM AMAZED how hard it is to use the technique of imagining when I am in a confrontational situation. Recently I missed an opportunity. My younger child attends a school that has the reputation of being progressive and diverse. Last year Sonja, an African American mother, and I formed a diversity committee for the school. This year at the first assembly we both were surprised to discover that the committee did not have the same status as the other committees, because parents had initiated it. We were both concerned that attaching the words "ad hoc" to the committee would send the message that diversity was not a major focus and concern of the school.

I attended a meeting to discuss the possibility of changing the committee status from ad hoc to a formal, essential committee in the school. As the board chair stated, a "no-brainer," right? Wrong. Fortunately (and unfortunately at times), the school prides itself on questioning everything. Sally, a white mother of an African American adopted son, interrupted the "no-brainer" statement and said that she believed that everyone was of one race, the human race. She shared her concern that a diversity committee would create division through the focus on differences. Over the last ten years, I have facilitated postplay discussions for approximately three hundred thousand people, and every time a variation of "We are all the same" has come up. I have watched the various actors in my theater troupe try to deal with the declaration of sameness with varying degrees of raw anger.

- A person would say, "I don't see your color." Edmonia's response was simply, and quite elegantly in my opinion, "Bullshit."

- Richard, who was from the Lummi nation, responded with: "See me. See my color. It is part of me. Love knows no color? No, loves sees color and loves all of me!"

- Eric, an African American man, responded with: "Now you want to take away my heritage, too? You don't see my color? Then how do you help me work through the fact that I was body-cavity-searched on my way to my high school prom because I 'fit the description'?"

My brain was filling with their responses at the same time I was realizing with horror that this woman, whose skin color was the same as mine, white, was raising her African American son to be just like her: white. She had never acknowledged his skin color as different from hers. He will have no preparation for the way some people will treat him. (Sonja, the co-chair of the diversity committee, told her African American son about Sally's way of raising her son. He said, "But Mom, that is so stupid. If someone says something to him because of his skin color, he won't know that they are stupid or mean. He'll think it's because of him.")

All of this was happening in my head as I tried to reason with Sally to change. Everyone in the room either joined her side or argued against it. There was a perfect conflict in the room, and because my blood was boiling, because she had ignited my defenses, my ability to try to imagine how she felt was nowhere within me. I now wish I had stopped and asked her if I could try to imagine how it felt to be her. "I wonder if you feel scared that talking about the issue will hurt your son. I would guess that you want the best for your son and want to protect him from any negative reactions."

If I had started by imagining how she might be feeling behind her words, she might have felt a connection. From that place of connection, the dialogue could have gone to a more productive place rather than become a polarized conflict. Our intentions were the same: to create a safe and nurturing world for our children. Unfortunately, she had not spent the time imagining how it might feel to be looked at as different in this society, because she did not have to; she felt painlessly included in terms of skin color. I missed a great opportunity during the meeting, but the good news is that it is not too late. Now I need to meet with Sally and begin the conversation again by using the technique of imagining how she feels. The result will, I hope, be a constructive dialogue on the subject of diversity.

The lesson in the previous experience is worth clarifying again and again. When we feel defensive we need the tool the most, but we may have the hardest time actually using it. Also, it is not productive to say, "If only I had said. . . ." I can always initiate a new conversation. "If only" is simply my cue to figure out how to improve the communication now and open up a constructive dialogue where both people can be challenged to grow.

Exercises:

- Think back to a moment when you could have responded with the imagination tool instead of defending yourself. Write your new response. If it has the potential to further your relationship with this person, contact him or her and share what you wrote.

CHAPTER FOURTEEN

It's the Little Things

WHAT about those mild irritations we may encounter when we are shopping or traveling? The technique of imagining how it feels to be the other person can be useful both for the customer and for the person who is the "customer service representative." I often forget to use the technique after my plane has been delayed for the third hour and I am talking to the ticketing agent, who really is not the one responsible for the San Francisco fog. I also wish that the many people who are on the receiving end of a customer's rage would simply try saying something like, "I imagine you must be feeling very angry right now... I am so sorry. How can I help?" instead of, "And what would you like me to do about that? Fill out the complaint form, please. Next?"

Last winter I was traveling to Denver with Marlaina and Tony, who are the two people who join me for *Not Just Ramps*, the play about access issues for people with disabilities. Tony and I perform the play and Marlaina, one of the people I portray in the show, conducts a workshop following the play. Marlaina is a wonderfully up-front woman who travels constantly for business. She leads awareness workshops and trains people who are blind or vision-impaired to use adaptive strategies. Tony has played a wide variety of roles on stage and television. He knows no performance fear but he does have acrophobia, a fear of heights. Whenever we travel, Tony needs to stay close to the first floor, and Marlaina, although she does not need a room specifically designed for people with disabilities, does need to be on the first floor so she can take Madelyn, her guide dog, outside easily.

Tony, Marlaina, and I arrived at a well-respected, historic hotel in Denver. After a long day of flying, we began the check-in ritual, and everything started to unravel. First the hotel clerk put me in a room designed for disabled accessibility and Marlaina in a room far from any exit. Tony was given a room on the fourteenth floor. I went back to the desk and asked for a different room, and Marlaina was reassigned to my old room, which, of course, was nowhere near an exit. Tony was then moved to the first floor near an exit and was finally joined by Marlaina, who got the room next to his room. I opened the door to my second room and found the nonsmoking room filled with that old smoke smell. I called the front desk and the clerk reluctantly agreed to move me into a *smoke-free* nonsmoking room after assuring me that my nose was lying. I fell onto my bed, thinking how we must have looked like the Marx Brothers with doors opening and closing and no one ever ending up in the right place.

The next morning, as we were checking out, we politely gave some feedback to a woman at the front desk about the room assignment mixups. If the clerk had used the technique of trying to imagine how we might have felt, I would not be writing about this experience. The mixup was just a *little thing* that became so much bigger because of how the employee was trained to respond. We explained the problem of assigning me to an accessible room when it should have been kept open for someone with a physical disability who might have needed it. We then described the ritual of room switching that took us about forty-five minutes to perform after a five-hour flight. The hotel clerk put on an artificial smile and said somewhat automatically: "I am sorry for the inconvenience; please fill out a feedback form located on the table behind you."

Each of us took a deep breath. We began to explain the room situation in a bit more detail, hoping that she would acknowledge our complaints. My biggest hope was that she would tell us that she would discuss our experience with other desk clerks in order to avoid repeating the problem with future hotel guests. However, I was willing to settle for a reply that at least implied that she had heard us. After our second try she repeated the statement, "I am sorry for the inconvenience...." I felt my body temperature rise and was ready to explain our check-in experience yet again, when Tony said, "Fine, we'll fill out the feedback form." We filled out the form, describing how the front desk clerks responded to complaints. If only the clerk had simply said, "That must have been awful for you. I imagine you must have felt frustrated after such a long flight. I will make sure your feedback is given to the manager."

If she had used the tool of imagining how it must have felt to be the three of us instead of repeating the "feedback form" statement, we would have felt we had been heard, and our frustration would have been diffused. It was just a *little thing*, but without her attempt to connect with our feelings of frustration, we left the hotel feeling less than enthusiastic about future stays there.

When Tony, Marlaina, and I travel together we seem to attract hotel "issues." Several months after the Denver hotel experience we found ourselves at an inexpensive hotel in Southern California. The government agency that hired us to do training had a low budget for travel expenses. The three of us were checking out of the hotel on our way to the presentation of *Not Just Ramps*. The desk clerk handed me a bill with fourteen dollars' worth of phone calls that I had not made. I told the clerk that I had not made the calls. She asked me how I could prove the calls were not mine. I showed her my cell phone as evidence that I would not need to use the hotel phone. I also pointed out that I had checked in after the phone calls were made. The clerk said she still did not know if the calls were my responsibility. All three of us at this point were becoming angry that my integrity was being questioned. The situation continued to deteriorate when the desk clerk put me on the telephone with the hotel manager. The manager kept restating the policy that I was responsible for the telephone calls. We left the hotel with the phone calls still on my bill and charge card. The manager said he would credit my card if they proved I had not made the long-distance telephone calls.

As we got in my car, we looked at each other a little guiltily. Tony said, "I guess that might have gone differently if we imagined what they must go through at that hotel. I bet people rip them off all the time." Tony was right. The desk clerk might have been friendlier if I had imagined her point of view out loud. She was trying to enforce an accepted policy at the hotel. If I was correct, then that meant there was an employee or a previous guest who was in effect stealing from the management. She also did not have the power to ameliorate the situation. I realized that the lack of resolution would have been more acceptable to me, too, if she had simply said, "I imagine that you might be feeling frustrated because it sounds as if I am questioning your honesty. I would hate that, too. Unfortunately, we still have to go through certain steps before we can resolve this." I immediately would have let go of feeling unjustly accused.

What happened at the hotel was a little incident in the big scheme of things, but our experience illustrates how small conflicts can escalate. Both parties to the conflict, the hotel and the three of us, were unwilling for a moment to imagine how the other party was feeling. I was busy feeling unjustly accused and the hotel staffers were busy feeling as if another customer was trying to steal from them. Just a slight adjustment in both positions would have resulted in a professional and courteous interaction.

Why is it so hard to remember to imagine how the other person is feeling when we are hooked emotionally? For me, a major reason is my need to be right rather than to do whatever it takes to solve a problem. Maybe it is just a matter of practice, practice, and more practice.

Exercises:

- Think back to your most recent argument with someone when you felt that he or she just needed to understand your position in order to agree with you. Replay the scene in your mind with a new response from you. This time begin with, "Can I try to imagine how it feels to be you right now?"

CHAPTER FIFTEEN

To Do It or Not to Do It

IF ONLY it were so easy. I have been aware of the power of imagining how it feels for twenty-two years. I even took a class in it. How often do I try to imagine how it feels to be another person in real life?

I have used the imagination technique at least three times outside the workshops—not exactly an impressive number. I am great at applying the technique in the workshop setting. Professionally and personally I approach any conflict that arises in a group situation with my tool. I have a long list of examples of times when it has been successful. For some reason, though, applying the tool in personally charged encounters with an individual is another story. For the most part, I either forget to imagine or resist imagining how it feels to be my husband because I am so invested in being right and maintaining my ground. Ironically, if I did step out of my position and imagine how it felt to come from his perspective, I would not lose anything. There is a strong possibility that I would help create a deeper understanding between us because my attempt to imagine how it feels to be him would invite him to reciprocate. One time when I let go of defending my position and imagined how it felt to be him, there was a wonderful result.

I was in my husband's truck, sitting in the passenger seat on the verge of boiling over. He was saying the typical words (typical for many, if not most, people in a relationship): "There you go again. You always have to be in control. I know what you really meant!" Normally I would have come back with: "Whoa, wait a minute, who has to be in control all the time? That's not what I meant at all, you've got it backwards."

I still do not know why I did not go to my usual defensive place, but that one day I stepped over it and said, "Can I try to imagine how it must have felt to be you when you heard me say blah, blah, blah? . . ."

It was like the silence that happens when the electricity goes out. No one knows exactly what to say or do, or even what happened, at first. I was ready for my husband to respond with even more anger, not loud silence. He was stumped. He looked at me and said, "What?" He seemed confusedly off-guard. "Uh, sure, go ahead."

And then I did. I stumbled over my words trying to imagine how he felt. There was no obligation to prove I was right or wrong; instead I focused on really trying to get it. The anger was gone and we were able to get through the argument almost painlessly. In a few minutes I asked him to do the same thing. "Can you try to imagine how it must have felt to be me?" He did. We reached a new understanding of each other and discovered that we had almost wasted several hours arguing over mistaken assumptions.

The tool worked! Why is it so hard consistently to use the tool of imagining how it feels to be other people?

- I feel fear; I am afraid of imagining how it feels to be them because I do not want to be them. My biggest fear is becoming the person with whom I am most angry, so why in the world would I try to imagine what it is like to be him or her?

- I am too invested in being right or good; I want the person to know where I was coming from so he or she knows I had good intentions. I want other people to know what I was thinking, because if they knew that they would know I was right.

- I *am* right. My opinions are very important to me. I have spent years forming them, so to let them go even temporarily is scary. The fear is that if I let anything different leak into my view of the world, I would have to question my whole value system. In one of my earlier disagreements with my husband, he blurted out, "You have opinions, but I am right." We both laughed, ending the argument. In the heat of an argument, though, I find myself agreeing with his statement.

- In order to imagine how it feels, I have to touch my own pain. I prefer to feel righteously angry than to feel my own pain.
- It is hard to do. I might have to fumble as I struggle to try to imagine how it feels. I would rather sound together and radiate my "personal power."

As adults we have been brainwashed to believe that mistakes are reserved for our children. We should know better and be close to perfection. We avoid mistakes and in the process avoid all possibility of learning from each other. Actually, it is in the moments when there is conflict or a perceived offense that the potential of creating a deeper connection is greatest.

If I go to my workplace determined to avoid saying the wrong thing, I will avoid every possible point of connection with my coworkers. I believe it is crucial that we let go of the need to be perfect. Let us find the mistakes and congratulate ourselves when we make them because they offer an opportunity for connection and growth. A mistake, a moment when I am not "right" or I have said something that is perceived as "offensive," is an opportunity to deepen the trust and connection with my colleague, friend, or partner. By my trying to imagine how it feels to be him or her, we have the chance to find a more intimate connection with each other, rather than developing a new safe distance.

The technique of imagining how it feels to be the other person produces results that most people want: more connection, more productivity, less burnout, more inclusion, and, with our coworkers, friends, and family, more intimacy. The idea is simple, yet difficult to implement.

I was doing training for a joint conference put on by a car manufacturer and a union. About an hour after we were finished with the play and the discussion, a woman came up to me in the hall. She said, "It just occurred to me what you were saying in there about imagining how it feels to be other people. If we really did that, then we wouldn't need this conference. We wouldn't be here at all. It's so simple; why don't we just do it?"

We do not do it because we were never taught to do it. Small children have incredible imaginations. My daughter Elsa is always saying, "Okay, you be Angeline and I'll be your mother." Children naturally try on other people's shoes (and clothes, for that matter) all the time, metaphorically and literally. I laugh when I imagine adults engaging in the ritual my daughter often goes through when a friend comes over. They go into her room and immediately, without invitation, take off their clothes and begin to try on all the other possible outfits in the room. The process of imagining how it feels to be another person is natural and expected in children's play.

When school begins, the time for imaginative play decreases. Children learn to unlearn the skill of putting themselves in someone else's shoes. Perhaps it is a time-management issue. The teacher has to teach certain concrete skills and it would take too long if the children kept playing "let's pretend."

Not putting themselves in someone else's shoes also becomes a survival issue for some people. I once interviewed a group of teenagers about violence for a play I was writing. One young woman described to me in graphic detail how she kept hitting another girl's face until the girl was so bloody she had to go to the hospital. I blurted out, half in shock: "How could you do that? How do you think she must have felt? You put her in the hospital." She looked at me as if I were crazy and said, "Who cares how she felt? I don't really know and I don't care. All I know is that I was pissed." I knew at that moment that if she had been retaught the skill of imagination, she could not have "pounded the other girl's face in." It is much more difficult to inflict pain when you imagine how the pain might feel.

I have talked about the difficulty of applying the technique of imagining in an emotionally charged situation. The opportunities for diversity and inclusion lie in conflict- or tension-filled situations. Diversity challenges assumptions and complacency, and therefore is not inherently easy to achieve. I believe we will never get beyond the need for diversity trainings and conferences until we have practiced the "tool of connection" so much that we automatically use the technique of imagining in a situation in which our buttons are being pushed.

I have practiced the tool of connection through imagining so much in group situations that I now automatically use it. I believe I have become a much more effective communicator because of this re-acquired skill. (Note that I am saying this regarding group situations; I have not fully mastered it in one-on-one encounters, an observation to which my husband can attest.)

At a recent meeting, several people confronted me about some hard issues. Unconsciously, I responded to each person by incorporating where he or she was coming from before sharing my perspective. A potentially loaded situation became a fascinating discussion of communication and education, with neither side going into a defensive mode. I attempted to understand the other people's perspectives by imagining out loud how they might have been feeling. I felt free of having to defend my position. The result was a discussion free of anger, in which we all learned more about one another. The tool of connection works both on a large scale and in direct conflict.

Exercises:

- Think of a conflict between two groups of people. The conflict can be one you are personally involved in or it can be on a national or even global scale. Imagine what would happen if both sides began the negotiations with statements starting with, "I am going to try to imagine what you may be feeling and thinking . . ." Finish their statements.

CHAPTER SIXTEEN

How to Practice the Tool of Imagining

TIME for a bit of hands-on work. I have developed a simple exercise that allows people to practice the technique of imagining how another person is feeling. In my workshops I have people pair up so they can answer five questions out loud about someone in their life with whom they are in conflict. I hope that throughout this book you have stopped to apply the tool to people and situations in your everyday life. Here is another chance. The following is an exercise you can do with a friend or by yourself.

The Exercise

The first step is to pick someone in your life, a family member or someone you work with, who really pushes your buttons—in other words, a person with whom you come in contact who irritates you or even angers you by his or her words or how that person lives. Okay, I bet that took about three seconds. Now on a piece of paper, out loud to yourself, or to a partner, answer the following questions. It is important that you find a way to verbalize or write your answers to the following questions so the words do not just float around inside your head.

1. What do I *not* like about (name) ? This is a fun question because normally we do not allow ourselves the freedom to answer this question out loud or on paper.

Please allow yourself to have fun and be completely honest.

2. What do I think about what ___(name)___ thinks? This question allows you to elaborate on the first question. I find that one of the main things I do not like about someone is his or her opinions. I have plenty of opinions about other people's opinions. Another way to ask this question is: What is your opinion of ___(name)___'s opinion?

3. What is your theory about ___(name)___? Intellectually analyze why you think this person behaves the way he or she does.

4. What makes me sad, mad, and scared about ___(name)___? Try not to think too much before you answer this question. Start a sentence with: "I am sad about; I am scared of." See what comes up. Try to respond from your emotional side rather than your cognitive thought process.

The final question requires an introduction. This question needs to come from a place different from the last question. The question requires that you do not answer spontaneously from an emotional place. If you find that the answer is coming out quickly and easily, you are probably cheating. (I will clarify this below.)

5. How do I imagine it feels to be ___(name)___?

If you answer the question quickly, it may sound a bit like this: "I imagine he or she feels superior to other people." Most people do not approach the day with the desire to feel superior to others. Equating your perception of their superior airs with their internal processes is simply disguising your assumptions with "feeling" words. There is a feeling and a perceived reality underneath the impression you may be getting. Answering this question is difficult and may involve discomfort. The discomfort that arises in imagining what it is like to be in another person's shoes is where the learning happens. You need to go deeper into your own experience and inner process to imagine truly how it might feel to be another person. The question is not easy to answer but the journey will be enlightening and rewarding.

Complete this exercise using several different people in your life. What did you discover about yourself and the other people? I have done this exercise on my own using various people I have known. My discoveries may or may not be similar to yours. I have noticed that the person I pick is usually someone whom I do not want to be like in any way. I answer the fourth question with: "I am scared of being her/him." My fear is what stops our communication. If I am scared of being like the other person, why would I think of trying to imagine how it feels to be him or her? Most of the time I conveniently forget about the tool of imagining because I simply do not want, on any level, to be like the other person. The result of my fear is that instead of trying to create a positive communication experience, I put up with the person and in effect ignore him or her. If I stay clearly in my anger, irritation, or fear, my behavior begins to be perceived by the other person the same way I perceive his or her behavior. The other person might think I feel superior because I am ignoring him or her. In other words, if I am too scared to imagine how it feels to be someone because I do not want to be him or her, I become that person, at least in behavior.

I perceive Louise as snobby. If I allow my assessment of Louise to end at the word "snobby," as opposed to trying to imagine how it feels to be her, then I may start to avoid her. I do not want to be with someone who appears snobby. Louise could easily label my avoidance behavior as "snobby." By not trying to imagine how it feels to be her, I end up acting just like her. My biggest fear comes true. I become Louise in terms of my perceived behavior.

Another exercise that you can use to strengthen the imagination muscle is to imagine how it would feel to live in a society where everything is reversed.

- For instance, all the television health and beauty aid commercials are cast with people who are not the typical blonde, twenty-something models. Perhaps the spokesperson for body lotion is a black woman with a disability.

- The congressional hearings you see on television are predominantly made up of people of color who talk openly about their same-sex spouses, with only a smattering of white heterosexual males who talk about the classic two-child, two-car family.

- The news articles you read about the latest murder or robbery only mention the suspect's skin color and ethnicity when that person is white or Euro-American.

- Whenever you go into a store, the security people follow you around (unless, of course, you already experience this because of your skin color or age).

- In a restaurant, the waitperson has already brought all the orders for the other tables of people who look different from you, even though you arrived half an hour before they did.

This list could go on and on. Pick moments in your life when you take for granted how you are treated and ask the question, "What if it were the opposite?"

At the end of the primary season for the 2000 presidential election, I saw pictures in the newspaper of Al Gore and George Bush, the two major-party candidates. The pictures were striking to me because the candidates looked almost identical. Each picture showed a white male in his mid- to late forties, with the same haircut, the same red tie, the same white shirt, and the same blue suit. As I studied the pictures, I was amazed that an election in the year 2000 had two almost identical-looking people who both come from the ethnic group that has traditionally held most of the political power in this country. I was a bit shocked by the pictures because they were such a graphic illustration of who still holds the political power in the two major parties and the government of the United States.

I showed the pictures to my husband and asked him to study them while imagining how it felt to be a woman from a different ethnic group who frequently had to choose between people who rarely looked like her in terms of skin color, gender, and other attributes. He was instantly able to imagine some of the pain and injustice a person might feel. Then I asked him to imagine that the pictures were of two African American women. I continued by saying that African American women were usually the only people whom the country elected to political office. The women came from the group of people he most often saw in the media and in positions of power. His reaction surprised me. He became angry and agitated. He told me he did not like using his imagination that way because it brought him to a place of hopelessness and rage. The hopelessness led to him feeling so overwhelmed that he found it extremely difficult to imagine any constructive way to change the situation. He felt that the first scenario, imagining how it might feel to see the two white males if he were someone who was not white and male, was more productive because he became more compassionate toward the person who was not represented. The compassion led to a feeling in him of wanting to confront the representational injustice in our society.

We continued to explore the differences in his reactions. I talked about the value of connecting to the hopelessness and rage he experienced in the second scenario when he changed the images in his mind to those of individuals who did not look like him in terms of gender and skin color. He wanted to know what value there was in his feelings of rage and hopelessness, because those feelings did not lead to him to want to confront the injustice. I believe the tool of imagining gave him valuable insight both ways. In the first scenario he was able to connect with the injustice in a way that led him to want to confront the inequity. The second scenario allowed him to imagine the level of rage people can reach when they are not included.

If we continue to ignore the possibility of rage and hopelessness that exclusion can cause in people, then the people who are left with those feelings will feel even more disconnected. The feeling of disconnection adds to the feeling of exclusion and will increase the levels of rage and hopelessness. The tool of imagining how it feels to be another person allows us to connect to all kinds of feelings, many of which may not appear productive or comfortable. The result of trying to imagine a person's rage is that it will, I hope, lead to a constructive dialogue rather than to behavior that may continue to fuel the rage.

Several years ago I saw the film *The Color of Fear*,[3] which was created as a tool for diversity training. The film was made by Lee Mun Wah, a facilitator and documentary filmmaker, who brought ten men from five different ethnic groups together for three days to explore their feelings and experiences of racism. There was a white man in the group who constantly told the people of color in the room that things could not really be so bad as they said. Finally, one African American man started yelling things like: "Shut up! Just stop talking! Let me have my pain! You have no right to take away my pain! You'll never know what it's like to be a black man." The continual attempts by the white man to deny the African American man's pain wore the second man's defenses down to the point where he was in a state of nonviolent rage. The white man began to cry. He confessed that he could not handle anyone else being in pain because he had not been allowed as a child to express his pain. He acknowledged the rage, anger, and pain he heard in the African American man. The result of his acknowledgment was relief. The African American man no longer needed to rage to be heard. If our fears keep us from imagining how it feels to be angry at the exclusion caused by racism or sexism or homophobia, then the anger will only increase.

Please try all the different ways of imagining how it might feel to be someone different from you, whether you imagine that everything is reversed around you or you imagine that you are a different person who does not see anyone like you in the media and your environment. In either approach there is valuable insight to be gained, which will lead to a constructive process of communication. The more you practice these imagination exercises, the easier it becomes to use the technique of imagining

---

[3] *The Color of Fear* by Lee Mun Wah, available through Stir Fry Seminars and Consulting, Inc., Calif.

how it feels to be someone different from you and so to transform your interactions with the people you work with and the people in your life.

CHAPTER SEVENTEEN

Will the Technique of Imagining Cure Me of My Prejudices?

No.

CHAPTER EIGHTEEN

Whadaya Mean, No?

(IF CHAPTER 17 was the one you reluctantly committed to reading before tomorrow, you lucked out.)

The technique of imagining does not cure me of any of my prejudices. If it did, then I would be on my way to the White House via the United Nations with my cure.

In the last ten years of performing plays that illustrate the tool of imagining how it feels to be other people, I have become more aware than ever of the biases and prejudices I learned growing up in this country. I was raised in a family of privilege where I was taught that my ethnic background and family lineage meant that I was special. In the words of my mother, when I interviewed her for *Not until You Know My Story,*

> I do know that a number of people in my race have had enormous advantages in education that go back generations. And I think from that we derive something that is very special, that we should cherish, and be very proud of. I think that having educated parents and grandparents before you is a great help. I think this privilege will come in time for black people.

I watched a lot of television and movies as a child. I was subtly conditioned to feel fear when I saw the color black, or sad when I saw someone in a wheelchair, or better than someone who had less money, or even slightly sickened by the idea of two women kissing each other. I flinched as I wrote those last statements because even though I know intellectually that they are ridiculously wrong, emotionally a part of me still resonates with those misconceptions.

The bad news is that the tool of imagining cannot exorcise my prejudices. The good news is that the tool can change my focus by allowing me to step out of my own prejudices and experience the world from a different perspective. If I notice one of my prejudices taking shape in my mind about someone, I can shift my focus from my prejudice to trying to imagine how it feels to be that person as he or she talks with me. If I am using the tool, then my focus is on the other person rather than on my prejudices.

Even if I am not aware of a prejudice, I may be thinking, "Look at me, here I am talking comfortably with this big black man who would have intimidated me before I started doing diversity work. Wow, I sure have made a lot of progress." If I am saying that to myself while the man is talking with me, then I am obviously not really hearing all of what he is saying. Again, the tool of imagining allows me to participate fully in a constructive dialogue with a person whom I perceive to be different from me. When I try to imagine how it feels to be him while he is telling me about his thoughts or experiences, then all my focus is on him, not on my need to pat myself on the back for working through my prejudices.

The tool of imagining does not eradicate all the "-ism"s, but it does allow me the opportunity to respond in a new way. My prejudices cannot inform my response to a person or a situation when I am actively trying to imagine how it feels to be another person.

When I facilitated postplay discussions with the G.A.P. Theater Company in schools, I never tried to imagine how it felt to be people who held points of view that I considered "wrong." I had developed a strong prejudice against anyone who had what I judged to be an intolerant view about a group of people. A father of a high school student stood up and said: "Your group has an agenda. You want these students to accept homosexuality when my religion tells me it is wrong. What gives you the right to come here and disrespect my religion?" I basically ended the dialogue as quickly as possible by thanking him for sharing his perspective. I refused to enter into a dialogue with him. If I had used my tool of imagining, I might have said, "I imagine you might be feeling angry and fearful that we may be trying to influence your or your child's belief system. I wonder if you fear that you or your child may experience feeling persecuted for your religious beliefs."

At that point, the father might have felt safe sharing his fears of persecution and isolation. I might have been able to elicit similar feelings from one of the actors who often shared his fears of persecution and isolation because of his sexual orientation. If I had been willing to try to imagine the father's feelings as part of the process, the anger the father left with might have been transformed into a feeling of connection with a gay person who felt similar feelings of fear and isolation.

The tool of imagining how it feels to be another person begins a process that forces me to create a constructive interaction rather than stop any interaction because of my judgment and prejudice.

CHAPTER NINETEEN

The Assignment

OCCASIONALLY, a participant in one of my corporate trainings will question whether the tool of imagining how it feels to be another person will actually make any difference when it comes to changing people's prejudices. When I first began to do diversity trainings ten years ago, I would try to answer the question with righteous adamancy: "If we could truly imagine how it feels to be other people, then there would not be any suffering in the world caused by discrimination." Professor Julius Lester's words, with my addition of "caused by discrimination," would come out of my mouth with passion. After the workshop I would begin to doubt what I was saying. I would think, "Come on, Carrie, who are you kidding? Putting yourself in other people's shoes will change the world? Here you go again. Trying to change the world. It's a simple idea that people probably have already tried." Self-doubt would instantly melt my confident facilitator/actor persona.

Now I answer the question differently. I do not proclaim that the act of imagining how it feels to be another person is the answer to eliminating the pain caused by discrimination. Actually, I do not believe in definitive answers to almost any social problem now. I think I finally get the beauty of what the Dalai Lama was saying when he came to speak at Amherst College in 1979 when I was a senior there. He spoke in our new gymnasium, where two thousand people were packed into the bleachers. People had come from all over western Massachusetts to hear him share his wisdom. Before his speech began, people were asked to write questions for him on index cards. At the end of his speech he read aloud the first one on the pile: "You are a very wise and spiritual man who has experienced more than most people will ever know in their lifetime. You have obviously found the secret to living a life filled with great joy and peace. What is the secret to life and the universe?"

I was not alone in leaning forward in my seat, poised to be bathed in the Dalai Lama's wisdom. He nodded his head, indicating that he understood the question. I waited, holding my breath so as not to miss one word. A little smile flickered in his eyes and mouth. He said, "I don't know." He was ready for the next question. I laughed, without knowing why until several years ago. There is no such thing as "one answer" or "one cure" for most anything. Life is about accepting change and enjoying the process change creates.

The act of imagining how it feels to be someone else is the first step in a dialogue. I know the tool of imagining will lead to a constructive process, but I do not know what the outcome will be. It is a little like what I imagine the thrill of skydiving is like. You just have to take a step off the plane and suddenly you are in the middle of a whole new experience every time you do it. When I say to someone, "Can I try to imagine how it feels to be you?" I am taking that step off the plane. I actually feel a combination of thrill and fear because I have no idea where the conversation will lead. When I ask people if I can imagine how they might be feeling after they share feeling offended or hurt by a prejudiced remark, I will see anything from smug self-confidence to shock register on their faces. In the next moment, as I begin to stumble over my words in imagining their feelings, I watch the confidence or the shock melt into trusting engagement. I feel alive and challenged as I really try to imagine their perspective. I often feel glimmers of pain that resonate with experiences I have gone through. I feel as if I am growing and making a real connection with the other person. Does it change the world? No. Does it change him or her? Maybe. Does it change me? Yes, every time.

As an actor and diversity trainer, I have spoken with a lot of people from major corporations in this country. In every discussion I encounter the same situation. The managers, executives, and employees I have met consider themselves to be good, empathetic people, and yet most of them have never really tried to imagine how it feels to be someone else who may have a different or conflicting perspective. A lot of people have been taught to use the words "I hear you saying . . . ," but these correct words are where, more often than not, the communication ends. Paraphrasing and repeating back what a person has said often leaves out the emotional meaning and impact of that person's statement and experience.

In one of my first presentations of *Not until You Know My Story*, I was working with senior-level managers who on the average had been with the company for more than twenty years. At the end of the session, one man who appeared to be in his early sixties said:

> I have been here for thirty years and have always considered myself an open-minded, conscientious employee and supervisor, but I don't think I have ever really done what you are talking about. It's actually kind of hard to do but I think it has value. I am going to try it.

And now, I dare you to do just that. The assignment is:

Try it. Try to imagine how it feels to be someone else who is different from you in some way. Try to imagine how it feels to be the person who expresses offense after a statement you made or a joke you told. Try to imagine how it feels to be the person who irritates you and pushes your buttons. Try to imagine how it feels to be the person who is so quiet that you have a hard time feeling anything toward him or her. Pick a person who is different from you in physical appearance, belief, or orientation to the world. Imagine how it must feel to experience the feeling of exclusion or discrimination subtly or blatantly on a daily basis simply because of who you are, how you live, or what you believe.

The title of the first play I wrote on racism for G.A.P. came from the phrase "The hurt of one is the hurt of all. The honor of one is the honor of all." The quote came from a conference of Native Americans that was held at the University of Lethbridge in 1981. I took the quote with me on a trip to Mexico in 1991 and wrote lyrics to the final song of the play *The Hurt of One* while sitting on the top of an ancient Mayan ruin. Imagining how it feels to be someone else is about human connection and sharing a person's pain in order to become part of the solution. I end this book with the lyrics; imagine how it feels to be on the receiving end of exclusion and discrimination.

The Hurt of One

When a growing mind is not given the chance
And only certain people can join in life's dance
When a person born with a different face
Is not included in the human race

The time has come for us to heed the call
The hurt of one is the hurt of all

When we praise the moments when we don't see hate
Instead of working each day not to discriminate
When the history books tell the victor's tale
And the message you hear is that you will fail

The time has come for us to heed the call
The hurt of one is the hurt of all

Afterword

IT IS SEPTEMBER 13, 2001, two days after the worst terrorist attack the United States has experienced. I have experienced the whole gamut of emotions: numbness, sadness, shock, horror, fear, and anger. What role does the tool of imagining have in this event?

I am trying to imagine how it feels to be an Arab. I do not have to look far to find a personal connection. As a white person I am connected by ethnicity to the annihilation of much of the Native American population. I am connected to the internment of Japanese Americans after Pearl Harbor. I am connected to the enslavement of Africans and the exploitation of those Africans to maintain the economy that sustained generations of my family. If I allow my anger and sadness to be directed indiscriminately at people from Afghanistan or Pakistan or any other country with a large Arabic population, then I must be willing to condone any prejudice directed at me because of the acts committed by people who share my skin color. Terrorism is not an ethnicity.

I imagine how it might feel to know someone who was killed by the acts of terrorism. I imagine how it might feel to be one of the people on one of the hijacked airplanes. I get physically ill even imagining this.

I also know that no matter how much radio I listen to, or how much I try to put myself in New York or D.C. or on a hijacked airplane, I will never really know what it was like. I can turn it off. The people involved could not turn it off, nor can the people who were connected with one or more of the innocent victims. And that is where this tool stops. It is a tool, it is not reality. I can and will use it to continue to guard against the prejudice that may surface because of my upbringing or events in my life. I can cross the bridge of connection to feel interconnected with people in New York, D.C., and around the world. The actions I take can be informed by my willingness to connect.

The bridge of connection will allow me to apply constructive action to my feelings. I also believe that if we are willing to meet on that bridge we can prevent any action we may take from being fueled by prejudice.

About the Author

CARRIE Gibson is an actor, playwright, author, and speaker. She has been doing anti-discrimination work through creating original theatrical documentaries and plays for the last fifteen years. For the past six years she has toured *Not until You Know My Story* and *Not Just Ramps* with her company, Had to Be Productions, around the country to businesses, government agencies, and educational institutions. Her most recent work, *I Don't See Color*, cowritten and performed with Anthony Curry, began touring in 2003. Ms. Gibson has a B.A. in English literature from Amherst College, a master's in psychology from Antioch University, and extensive theater training. She currently lives in Venice, California, with her husband and daughter. Her website is www.hadtobe.com.

Current Offerings

Not until You Know My Story is a one-woman play and training that includes the stories of fourteen characters based on actual interviews. The differences that are addressed include race, ethnicity, religion, sexual orientation, disability, gender, size, and privilege.

Not Just Ramps is a two-person play and training about physical, emotional, and societal access issues for a diverse group of people with disabilities, including blindness, spinal cord injury, deafness and hearing loss, A.L.S. (Lou Gerhig's Disease), cerebral palsy, breathing and vocal impairment, dyslexia, mental illness, and developmental disabilities.

I Don't See Color is a theatrical documentary and training in which a range of individuals share their stories, emotions, humor, and action steps related to skin-color privilege, prejudice, and responsibility.

Ms. Gibson can be contacted at carriegibson@earthlink.net.

* * *

"Imagine getting a diverse group of fourteen people together to talk honestly and openly about their personal experiences with the pain of discrimination based on race, ethnicity, religion, sexual orientation, disability, gender, size, and privilege. Throw in a stand-up comedy introduction to loosen up the audience and a woman who offers deep personal reflections about her own life of privilege and biases. Pull the elements together in a tightly woven, not-a-minute-wasted package. Follow with a discussion in which coworkers share personal experiences of discrimination and reflections on a level they haven't remotely approached in perhaps years of working together.

"If you can imagine all that, you have some idea of the power of Carrie Gibson's one-woman show *Not until You Know My Story.*"

—Betty King Buginas, *The West County Weekly*

Printed in the United States
35237LVS00007B/15